Poet in the
New World

POEMS, 1946–1953

Czesław Miłosz

NEW TRANSLATIONS BY ROBERT HASS AND DAVID FRICK
EDITED BY ROBERT HASS AND DAVID FRICK

An Imprint of HarperCollins*Publishers*

HarperCollins books may be purchased for educational, business,
or sales promotional use. For information, please email the Special
Markets Department at SPsales@harpercollins.com.

Ecco® and HarperCollins® are trademarks of HarperCollins Publishers.

FIRST EDITION

Foreword copyright © 2025 by Robert Hass

Designed by Patrick Barry

Library of Congress Cataloging-in-Publication Data
has been applied for.

ISBN 978-0-06-342299-5

24 25 26 27 28 LBC 5 4 3 2 1

In memoriam

D. F. 1955–2022

CONTENTS

INTRODUCTION

THIS WAS A PROJECT THAT, once it had been proposed, seemed irresistible: to document the imaginative development of one of the great poets of the twentieth century during the most dramatic and complex years of his life by translating all, or almost all, of the poems he wrote in those years. Most of his poems from an immense body of work produced across a violent century and its aftermath have been translated. For various reasons, many of the poems from this period had not, so the two of us, a scholar of Polish literature and a poet who had worked with Czesław Miłosz for many years, got to work.

The result is *Poet in the New World,* which gathers in English translation the poems Miłosz wrote between 1946 and 1950 when he served as diplomatic official for the newly formed government of Poland at the consulate in New York City for six months, and then as cultural attaché to the embassy in Washington, DC, for four years. It concludes with translations of the handful of poems he wrote in Europe, mostly in Paris, in the tumultuous years between 1951 and 1953 when he broke with the Polish government and sought political asylum in France. In that fraught time he turned to prose to explain the choices he had made. The *Captive Mind,* which appeared in 1953, became one of the classic books on literature and the totalitarian imagination in the twentieth century, but its author thought of himself as a poet and understood that he had risked losing a relationship to his art, to his language, and to his readers by exiling himself from Poland.

Some background: In 1944 Miłosz had walked away from a city in ruins. Something like 80 percent of the buildings in Warsaw had been destroyed by the German army as they withdrew from the city, an act of pure vengeance ordered by Hitler; 150,000 Polish citizens, most of them young, had been killed in the uprising against the Germans who were retreating from the city as the Russian army approached. When their neighborhood began to be torched on August 11, Miłosz and his partner (later his wife), Janina Dłuska, and Janka's mother fled to the outskirts of the city, where they were caught by a patrol of the German army and put in an internment camp. Later, he would tell the story of seeing a group of boys playing football near the camp fence. He beckoned them over and asked them to deliver some notes, one of which reached a nun from a local convent, who then pleaded successfully with the German commandant for their release. They moved east on foot—away from the German army, toward the Russian army— and almost immediately fell victim to thieves who took what money and valuables they were carrying. In September they found lodging in a village in return for work digging in the field. Years later, beyond the turmoil, he would remember it as a moment when he had stepped out of history:

> *I rolled a cigarette and licked the paper.*
> *Then a match in the little house of my hand.*
> *And why not a tinderbox with flint?*
> *The wind was blowing. I sat by the road at noon.*
> *Thinking and thinking. Beside me, potatoes.*

By early November they headed south and east and reached the estate of friends in a village near Krakow, where they and other lodgers found refuge.

In Krakow, relatively unscathed by the war (but an hour's drive from Auschwitz) and under Soviet control, what was left of Polish society was beginning to put itself back together. Miłosz was able to join a newly formed writers union, was able to participate in a poetry reading (the young Wisława Szymborska, another future Nobel laureate, was in the audience). In the early spring he visited what remained of Warsaw with his friend, the novelist Jerzy Andrzejewski. (See "In Warsaw": this book begins with a poem Miłosz wrote about the trip.) That summer and fall he was able to work on the poems he had written during the war and found time to apply for a diplomatic post in the new government. In November he received an appointment to serve in the United States. In December he flew to London where, among other things, he had lunch with T. S. Eliot, whom he had translated. He received a book of his own poems of the war years just before he boarded the ship that would take him into a new life.

Miłosz arrived in New York on January 16, 1946, six months after the end of the war in Europe, four months after the surrender of Japan. He was thirty-five years old. His employers at the consulate in Manhattan had arranged for him and his wife an apartment on the Upper West Side, at 342 West 71st Street. The consulate was on Lexington and 67th, on the East Side, so his introduction to this new country must have been a walk across Central Park in the brisk winter air. It takes a while for the park to show up in the poems, and when it does, the scene is summer. Young men in uniform are sprawled on the lawn in the dark with their young women in their arms, watching an outdoor movie, and the flicker of the projector lights up the buildings along 5th Avenue and evokes in him the memory of his last look at Warsaw as it burned.

His first response to the United States, like that of many other visiting Europeans in this period, was at least a little defensive. This seems to have been especially so to those who had been removed from the ruin of European cities to the middle of Times Square. "Buildings this tall are nonsense!" he wrote to a friend not long after his arrival, "and all the neon is a cheap gimmick." Part of the fascination of the poems of these years is in watching his imagination simultaneously take on the extraordinary violence he had witnessed and the strange postwar United States that he was beginning to explore, while the tightening grip of the Soviet Union on Poland was slowly making his position in the Polish embassy untenable.

The Polish scholar Aleksander Fuit described Miłosz's situation this way:

. . .

> After all, the outstanding poet, the future author of *The Captive Mind*, decides to play in the United States the role of a diplomat of the People's Republic of Poland. This Polish citizen, after the experience of war, occupation, the imposition of a totalitarian system in his homeland, finds himself on the other end of the world, where historical experience seems to shape individual and collective attitudes only to a small extent. This witness to the brutal degradation of humanity, cruel Nazi terror, round-ups on the streets, executions, the Holocaust, the Warsaw Ghetto Uprising in 1943, the Warsaw Uprising in 1944, the total extermination of a city of more than a million residents, and the invasion of the Red Army—is confronted with a society for which the war happened somewhere far away, while respect for individual rights and for fundamental principles remains obvious and indisputable. The European, coming from the Old World that was ruined and impoverished by war, finds himself in the New World, which boasts of its prosperity, a far higher level of development, and forms of social and political organization little known to him.

Whatever his reservations, he threw himself into his work with characteristic diligence. In addition to reaching out to the Polish émigré community—which was very chary of and sometimes actively hostile to this poet in his role as a diplomat for Communist Poland, he reported in Polish on American newspapers and magazines like the *Partisan Review* and Dwight MacDonald's *Politics*. He had improved his English by translating Shakespeare and Browning and Eliot. Now he wrote essays on Ernest Hemingway, William Faulkner, Henry Miller; he translated poems by Wallace Stevens, introduced Polish readers to African American and Afro-

Caribbean poets, translated a selection of African American spirituals, noting the way the songs about the enslavement of the Jewish people in Egypt gave the enslaved a code in which to escape censorship (a subject sensitive enough in Poland that the editors printed the poems but not the commentary). He also translated Pablo Neruda, remarking that Spanish was easy if you knew French and that Polish poetry in the grayness of the postwar could use a little color. And he traveled, to a Bread Loaf conference, where he met Robert Frost, to New York and Detroit and Chicago to attempt to set up Polish studies programs at universities and libraries, to New Mexico and the West Coast with visual artists to promote Polish artists and Polish textiles. He acquired a car. He and his wife were able to explore the United States while he worked on his poems and wrote articles about his impressions of America for Polish journals. And he became father to his first son, Antoni. His appetite for work had always been enormous, and his superiors in the first few years commented on his diligence and imagination.

And yet he had begun to trouble his superiors. One of the poems he wrote—"Treatise on Morals," a twelve-page poem in rhymed couplets and the rhythm of a Kraków cabaret song—was published in a Polish literary journal and was disturbing to them. In 1949 he visited Warsaw on vacation and found the atmosphere grim. He had the impression that everyone he met, including old friends, averted their eyes in conversation and watched their words. Also that one could tell who had prospered and who had not in the postwar regime by the cut of their clothes and that he was dressed like the fortunate and well-placed. He returned to Washington, feeling that he could no longer do what he was doing. His superiors, meanwhile, reported that the poet was "ideologically totally alien." Defection, which he had begun to contemplate, meant cutting his relationship to Polish readers—death, it seemed, for a poet.

Back in Washington, he was told that he was being reposted to Paris, but was to return to Warsaw first. He left his wife and young son in the US to prepare for the move and flew first to Paris and then to Warsaw, where the authorities confiscated his passport. He appealed to friends, one of whom was well-placed enough to help him get him his passport and his assignment back. He flew to Paris where within weeks he defected, writing what was to become an infamous one-page essay titled "Nie" ("No") in a new Polish émigré magazine whose offices gave him a place to hide for several months, since he had no notion of how the Polish government would respond to his betrayal. The story gets told in detail in Andrzej Franaszek's *Miłosz: A Biography*.

Miłosz was not at first comfortable with the milieu in which he'd taken refuge. He thought of it, wrongly, as attached to a sentimental idea of an aristocratic Poland that was gone forever, but it proved to be welcoming and a lifeline. There was no question of his getting a passport to travel to the United States, where he'd been, officially, a Communist diplomat, and the émigré community in Paris wanted nothing to do with him for the same reason. By his own account he was isolated and very near the edge of madness, at moments assured that he'd made a catastrophically wrong decision, and what he did in the first ten months of 1951 was turn to prose and write *The Captive Mind*, which became an international bestseller and took its place among the classic books of the period about totalitarian politics, like Arthur Koestler's *Darkness at Noon* and George Orwell's *1984*. It also isolated him in France, where most writers and intellectuals (with the exception of Albert Camus) were solidly pro-Stalin. He wrote his first novel, *Seizure of Power*, in three months in the summer of 1952. The book won a literary prize, as *The Captive Mind* was published, and provided him with enough money to bring his wife and family—his wife had given birth to a second son—to Paris. This book ends with a poem, "Notebook: Bons by Lake Leman" set in the Swiss countryside at the time of their reunion.

This is the background to the story these poems tell about a poet finding his way in the wake of a catastrophic war and in a world that was just coming into being and already riven by conflicting ideologies. The poems written during these years were published in a volume titled *Swiatlo Dziennie* (*Daylight* or *The Light of Day*) in 1953 while he was settling into his life as an exiled writer, living with his family in a suburb of Paris and returning to a sense of his vocation as a poet, though he understood that he could no longer be published in Poland and that his poems were being removed from Polish anthologies. He himself wasn't very happy with the book he had assembled. In an interview in 1981, after he had won the Nobel Prize, he commented on it: "*The Light of Day* is not a very well-ordered collection; it's rather haphazard. It lacks a unifying principle. I'm not very fond of it as a whole; I write it off as a loss. The book's structure is chaotic because of my difficult personal situation and the pressure of the political atmosphere, which had been alienating me from poetry for a number of years."

Later, when he gathered collections of his poems for English translation, he chose to render only a handful of the poems from this period, and scholars have noticed that, when he was preparing the original volume, he tried at least three different ways of ordering the poems. Perhaps it's easier to see from here, seventy years later, the way in which these poems do have a unifying principle when they are organized more or less chronologically to tell the story of a poet recovering from a war of extraordinary violence, taking his bearings in a new world, and trying to locate and understand his task as a poet. That he had trouble giving the book an order isn't surprising. He tried out many stances, many tones. The poems are successively apocalyptic, satiric, surreal, elegiac, stunned with survivor guilt, hungry for a way forward. There are formal poems and poems that mock traditional forms. The centerpiece, the tour de force, from these years is the "Treatise on Morals," in which he tries to work out for himself and for Polish readers what morality has survived the war, or at least how not to lie to oneself in an uncertain and unpredictable time, a poem composed in a dance-hall rhythm so odd that it escaped the censors. Another European exile from this period, the philosopher and critic

Theodor Adorno, spent the war years in Pacific Palisades, a pleasant coastal neighborhood of Los Angeles, and it was he, looking back across the wreckage, who said, famously, that "to write poetry after Auschwitz is barbaric." What the poems in this period make clear is that this poet thought that it would be barbaric not to try.

— ROBERT HASS

1945, WARSAW

IN WARSAW

What are you doing here, poet, on the ruins
Of St. John's Cathedral this sunny
Day in spring?

What are you thinking here, where the wind
Blowing from the Vistula scatters
The red dust of the rubble?

You swore never to be
A ritual mourner.
You swore never to touch
The deep wounds of your nation
So you would not make them holy
With the accursed holiness that pursues
Descendants for many centuries.

But the lament of Antigone
Searching for her brother
Is indeed beyond the power
Of endurance. And the heart
Is a stone in which is enclosed,
Like an insect, the dark love
Of a most unhappy land.

I did not want to love so.
That was not my design.
I did not want to pity so.
That was not my design.
My pen is lighter
Than a hummingbird's feather. This burden
Is too much for it to bear.
How can I live in this country
Where the foot knocks against
The unburied bones of kin?
I hear voices, see smiles. I cannot
Write anything; five hands
Seize my pen and order me to write
The story of their lives and deaths.
Was I born to become
A ritual mourner?
I want to sing of festivities,
The greenwood into which Shakespeare
Often took me. Leave
To poets a moment of happiness,
Otherwise your world will perish.

It's madness to live without joy
And to repeat to the dead
Whose part was to be gladness
Of action in thought and in the flesh, singing, feasts,
Only the two salvaged words:
Truth and justice.

   —WARSAW, 1945

1946, NEW YORK AND WASHINGTON, DC

CHILD OF EUROPE

1

We, whose lungs fill with the sweetness of day,
Who in May admire trees flowering,
Are better than those who perished.

We, who taste of exotic dishes,
And enjoy fully the delights of love,
Are better than those who were buried.

We, from the fiery furnaces, from behind barbed wires
On which the winds of endless autumns howled,
We, who remember battles where the wounded air roared in
    paroxysms of pain,
We, saved by our own cunning and knowledge.

By sending others to the more exposed positions,
Urging them loudly to fight on,
Ourselves withdrawing in certainty of the cause lost.

Having the choice of our own death and that of a friend,
We chose his, coldly thinking: let it be done quickly.

We sealed gas chamber doors, stole bread,
Knowing the next day would be harder to bear than the day before.

As befits human beings, we explored good and evil.
Our malignant wisdom has no like on this planet.

Accept it as proven that we are better than they,
The gullible, hot-blooded weaklings, careless with their lives.

2

Treasure your legacy of skills, child of Europe,
Inheritor of Gothic cathedrals, of baroque churches,

Of synagogues filled with the wailing of a wronged people.
Successor of Descartes, Spinoza, inheritor of the word "honor,"
Posthumous child of Leonidas,
Treasure the skills acquired in the hour of terror.

You have a clever mind which sees instantly
The good and bad of any situation.
You have an elegant, skeptical mind which enjoys pleasures
Quite unknown to primitive races.

Guided by this mind you cannot fail to see
The soundness of the advice we give you:
Let the sweetness of day fill your lungs.
For this we have strict but wise rules.

3

There can be no question of force triumphant.
We live in the age of victorious justice.

Do not mention force, or you will be accused
Of upholding fallen doctrines in secret.

He who has power, has it by historical logic.
Respectfully bow to that logic.

Let your lips, proposing a hypothesis,
Not know about the hand faking the experiment.

Let your hand, faking the experiment,
Not know about the lips proposing a hypothesis.

Learn to predict a fire with unerring precision.
Then burn the house down to fulfill the prediction.

4

Grow your tree of falsehood from a small grain of truth.
Do not follow those who lie in contempt of reality.

Let your lie be even more logical than the truth itself,
So the weary travelers may find repose in the lie.

After the Day of the Lie gather in select circles,
Shaking with laughter when our real deeds are mentioned.

Dispensing flattery called: perspicacious thinking.
Dispensing flattery called: a great talent.

We, the last who can still draw joy from cynicism.
We, whose cunning is not unlike despair.

A new, humorless generation is now arising,
It takes in deadly earnest all we received with laughter.

5

Let your words speak not through their meanings,
But through them against whom they are used.

Fashion your weapon from ambiguous words.
Consign clear words to lexical limbo.

Judge no words before the clerks have checked
In their card index by whom they were spoken.

The voice of passion is better than the voice of reason.
The passionless cannot change history.

6

Love no country: countries soon disappear.
Love no city: cities are soon rubble.

Throw away keepsakes, or from your desk
A choking, poisonous fume will exude.

Do not love people: people soon perish.
Or they are wronged and call for your help.

Do not gaze into the pools of the past.
Their corroded surface will mirror
A face different from the one you expected.

7

He who invokes history is always secure.
The dead will not rise to witness against him.

You can accuse them of any deeds you like.
Their reply will always be sincere.

Their empty faces swim out of the deep dark.
You can fill them with any features desired.

Proud of dominion over people long vanished,
Change the past into your own, better likeness.

8

The laughter born of the love of truth
Is now the laughter of the enemies of the people.

Gone is the age of satire. We no longer need mock
The senile monarch with false courtly phrases.

Stern as befits the servants of a cause,
We will permit ourselves only sycophantic humor.

Tight-lipped, guided by reasons only,
Cautiously let us step into the era of the unchained fire.

—NEW YORK, 1946

TWO MEN IN ROME

Darkness begins at Castel Sant'Angelo,
At the globe's still point, where the Tiber unravels time.
The fading earth, touched by wind, breathes among the ashes.
One can hear the rustling of a lizard,
The scurrying of a mouse, and the weeping of the world.

As long as blood flows in the human body
And is alive with the love of other bodies,
It is possible to live in joy or despair.
But when the abstract void of the earth appears
And the time of farewell draws near,
The smell of leaves, the shape of clouds mean nothing.

My coat of royal purple won't save my wrinkled hands.
The pulse of time beats slowly in me
And the quick and the dead give their one speech
Now and for all the days to come.

I have heard the demand to feel pity,
But I can't summon the pity required,
In our small lives it is no more than a five-minute walk
From the child's cradle to the grave.

So why should I feel pity for those who perish,
Carry those small lives tenderly in the palm of my hand?
In the great twilight, bent over the first cause,
I quelled the pain in me and extinguished the delight.

At the globe's still point, where nothing changes,
There is a different compassion: of a human kind,
Begun there where the power of memory ends,
In the great shining quiet of the still point.

. . .

The clatter of sandals in the dark,
One strike on a mandolin, lengthening and fading,
Song of a soldier dreaming of Brooklyn
And the smell of mold from the river.

Let's go under the shadow of the colonnade
Where the fountain repeats its ancient motion
Where, on the stones, in the weak moonlight
Shapes of the earth appear, having been summoned.

An invisible theater floating in the air
And a lively song gathered from the summer night:
Ta tada tada.

A Cardinal, looking on, pinches his ring.
Beside him stands a shadow in cape and cowl.
They are the solitary onlookers in the darkness
And the lively rise and fall of song.

   . . .

A poet of this epoch doesn't bare his face
Because the creases drawn by terror would be revealed,
And, in the moonlight, the clenched teeth, the sneer.
The intricate music of words does not serve him,
As it served poets who aimed to express ecstasy.
He thinks coldly, calculates the distance to a clearing.

His dwelling has an echo in the mold of old foundations,
In intermittent sighs, in rust, a useless pen.
And everything is both simultaneous and stopped—
A second can open in him a spewing wound;
His century the sound of a shell at the bottom of the sea.

Caught between contradiction and contradiction,
He produces a new choice.
And what he chooses is never what it should have been.

Thunder in one's hand and in the valley the roar of the forest,
A man falling into a cemetery in the rocks.
And nothing remains. And always too little.

A memory postponed to the last hour,
An unnamed memory, forbidden to himself.
Pearls of childish tears in an avenue of maples,
At dawn on the shores of lakes smoking rushes
And deeds, my sad human deeds.

. . .

And there's the dancing girl.
Ta tada tada
From the mirrors of the night a timid foot emerges
And, bending down, her toes take the first step.

Slowly she draws up her knee
And the dark sex is visible, the mark distinguishing the human dead
From inanimate matter through the bygone possibility
Of procreation. It is masked by threads of beads
That sway.

She throws her hands upward, and her breasts
With the dark marks from which we sucked,
Where we nestled with our deceased mothers,
Precede her flight
To an invisible star.

Shaggy and sunken faces look at her.
Motionless, millions on millions
Chewing on breadcrusts found in the corner of the barracks
And she soars, fluttering, until suddenly, screaming,
Casting her arms down, she falls headfirst
In a quiet burst like a burst of magnesium
Onto the stony edge of a disused fountain.

. . .

I hear how laughter and crying rise
In that night that has neither beginning nor end.
Accursed Cardinal, let go of my hand.
Do you want me to stand forever
With my memory killed by that lunatic song,
Ready to be embalmed
In gilded dust, in the smoke of burning aloe?

I know that one pays for that mute staring.
When I was chanting Ovid and dreaming of laurels on my brow,
I was already swimming out on those somber waters
Where a crowd of sad figures rushes to the incantation.

Yes, I was a witness. But I was never reconciled.
No one living will tear assent from my lips.
Anyone faithful won't be conciliated.
If your Vatican lies broken
I will keep going, to bear in the windstorm
The *aurea aetas* from heart to heart.

. . .

When the stilts clatter,
When the procession of ragged overcoats,
Of the whites of eyes, unmoving like eyes of marble
When women tied their falling stockings with string
And bundles are carried by a strap across the forehead,
When old people mourn their final love
For a wooden doll or a packet of letters.

—NEW YORK, 1946

1947, WASHINGTON, DC

TO JONATHAN SWIFT

To you I address myself, dear Dean,
Asking for your good advice.
Since we meet infrequently,
I won't clothe myself in glory.

I see a greenish ocean break
Against a rocky shore. The long
White fingers of the surf set off
The emerald island handsomely.

A stone of dark violet shimmers
Over Ireland's peateries;
In houses under hooting owls,
Barley sputters in the stew.

Silver braid, a glint of wig,
And a goose pen draws a map—
Not in the way that people think—
For instruction and for art.

I followed it, sign after sign,
And found the shortcuts useful.
I visited the Brobdingnagians,
I skirted the Laputa Isles.

I also met the Yahoo tribe,
Living in their slavish fear,
A cursed brood of informers
Who adore their excrement.

My life broke into islands,
Through no choice of my own.
Though sea storms flushed my heart,
They did not empty it completely.

I did not wrap feigned blindness
Like a ribbon around my eyes
So a thorough anger now brightens
My numerous small duties.

You, my Dean, can indicate
How that strange liquid is conceived
That fills the empty inkpot up,
Darkening the blackest ink.

Teach me the secrets of your age,
Lest I wear the smooth-faced frown
Of those who lecture about Man
And whimper only in their sleep.

The prince, reflected in a mirror,
Wants only praise from poets' stories
And courtiers bowing low, and lower,
Rows of rumps of Whigs and Tories.

The prince, my Dean, is usually wrong,
Though he has reasons (of state) and strength
Behind him. One slip will pack him off
To where an index card consigns him.

Your home beneath the hooting owl
Where night pours down an Irish rain
Will long outlast the marble bust
And adulating laurel trees.

Here is what your lips have said:
The cause of man is not past hope.
Who thinks that history is consummation
Dies an uncomprehending death.

Courage, my son, hold to your ships.
Haul the comic fleet on ropes
And let the range of clouds avenge
The antlike kingdom's past mistakes.

As long as there are earth and heaven,
Prepare new havens for new towns.
Apart from that, there is no pardon.
I will persevere, my Dean.

—WASHINGTON, DC, 1947

SONG ON PORCELAIN

Rose-colored cup and saucer,
Flowery demitasses:
You lie beside the river
Where an armored column passes.
Winds from across the meadow
Sprinkle the banks with down;
A torn apple tree's shadow
Falls on the muddy path;
The ground everywhere is strewn
With bits of brittle froth—
Of all things broken and lost
Porcelain troubles me most.

Before the first red tones
Begin to warm the sky
The earth wakes up, and moans.
It is the small sad cry
Of cups and saucers cracking,
The masters' precious dream
Of roses, of mowers raking,
And shepherds on the lawn.
The black underground stream
Swallows the frozen swan.
This morning, as I walked past,
The porcelain troubled me most.

The blackened plain spreads out
To where the horizon blurs
In a litter of handle and spout,
A lively pulp that stirs
And crunches under my feet.
Pretty, useless foam:
Your stained colors are sweet,
Spattered in dirty waves
Flecking the fresh black loam
In the mounds of these new graves.
In sorrow and pain and cost,
Sir, porcelain troubles me most.

—WASHINGTON, DC, 1947

ON THE SONG OF A BIRD ON THE
BANKS OF THE POTOMAC

When the magnolias bloom
And the park is a splash of muddy green,
I hear your song on the bank of the Potomac
On evenings lulled to sleep by cherry petals.
Please pardon the absence of those emotions
That lead one back by force
To places and springtimes long forgotten
So that poets might seduce the young
With patriotic feeling, might press
The longing heart, coloring the muddle
Of childhood and youth in a blur of tears.
I find this unpleasant. Why should I
Recall Ponary, yellow with young leaves,
With the almond scent of Daphne shrubs,
Screams of the grouse echoing in the forest?
Why should I enter again the dark halls
Of King Sigismund August High School
Or prod the pines with a great whip
On the road from Jazuny, as Slowacki once did?

We played our games on the Mereczanka
Or played we were courtiers of King Władysław.
The story of our loves and our partings—
Or were they love songs of the Philomaths?—
I no longer recall. Bird, graceful bird,
You who sing to me today the same song
That an Indian hunter would have heard here
Standing with his bow on the deer path,
What can you know of the passing of generations,
Or of the succession of forms in the course
Of a single life? Those traces of my youth
Were not effaced by the momentum of the seasons
Only. I was witness to misfortunes, I know what it means
To cheat life with the coloring of memory,
I listen to your lovely tones with joy,
Here on the great earth Spring is renewing,
My home of a second: in it the world's beginning.
So sing! Shower the dew of song from the banks
Of the Potomac onto the pearl of its ash-gray waters.

—WASHINGTON, DC, 1947

THE SPIRIT OF THE LAWS

From the cry of children on the floors of stations beyond time,
From the sadness of the engineer of prison trains,
From the red scars of two wars on the forehead,
I awoke under the bronze of winged monuments,
Under the griffins of a Masonic temple
With the dying ash of a cigar.

It was a summer of plane trees in colonnades and pearls of birds
    poured from the dawn,
A summer of joined hands, of black, of violet,
A summer of blue bees, of whistles, of flames
And the tiny propellors of a hummingbird.

And I, with my pine anchor on a sandy plain,
With the silenced memory of dead friends
And the silenced memory of towns and rivers,
I was ready to tear out the heart of the earth with a knife
And put there a glowing diamond of shouts and complaints,
I was ready to smear the bottom of roots with blood
To invoke the names on their leaves,
To cover the malachite of monuments with the skin of night
And write down with phosphorus Mene Tekel Upharsin,
Shining with the traces of melting eyelids.

I could go to the riverside where lovers
Look at the remnants of games floating to the sea,
I could enter parking lots, iridescent soap bubbles
And listen to the laboring
Of the eternal humanity of muted notes,
Of industrious, agile male muscles
Over a hot butterfly of carmine.

Gardens hopping down to the bottom of ravines,
The national dances of gray squirrels
And the white laboratories of winged infants
Always growing up in a different epoch,
The shine, the juice, the rouge of the day
All of it
Seemed to be the beginning of the sun on yellow plains,
Where in railway stations at a wobbling table,
Sitting over an empty glass, their faces in their hands,
Are the sad engineers of prison trains.

    —WASHINGTON, DC, 1947

A REMINDER

We passed by islands,
Springs came in turn.
Girls brought the fuzz
Of peaches on their cheeks.
Sparks of neon flickered
through the leaves of the trees.
Streams of a guitar echoed
In the mountain's forests
And lips, joined, lit
By the meter of a taxi,
Rode over asphalt
Past the wings of monuments,
At the airports the night
Shone in the embrace of lamps.
And Greece, Greece,
Who here remembers that?

Our world undoubtedly
Changes for the better.
The earth yields
To the shiny machine.
Misfortune visits
The unfortunate lands.
Each of us is fortunate,
For we are free from guilt.
Fate, out hunting, will lose
The scent that led us here.
An ocean divides us from
The evils of Europe,
And Liberty gives a sign
To the travelers on the boats.
About Greece, Greece,
Who here remembers that?

In the leaves children sang
And listened to their echoes.
Combines glided in rows
Across a thousand miles
Of ripe wheat under the sun.
The singing cicadas
Glistened on the apples
And cisterns gathered
A silver radiance in the deltas.
To helmsmen the contours
Of cities appeared white
And a taut network
Of aerial paths quivered.
About Greece, Greece,
Who remembers that?

That somewhere far away
The war still burns?
This happens only
Among benighted mountain folk
Who consider a sheepskin cape
A great treasure and reckon
Such miserable lives cheaply.
It's the lot of barbarians
To settle scores with blood.
Since law is alien to them,
And so they are ready to perish
At some operative's command.
Greece, Greece,
Who remembers that?

Rain fell on Mount Olympus,
The wind carried clouds of smoke,
And the sound of the bullets
Played brief hymns serially.
The echoes of cannons
Kept track of the hours
For those who don't know
How to doze without guilt.
But they, though guilty,
Gave what they had:
A cape, a string of beads,
The coral color of lips.
They went into the untilled earth
And rain washes away their brands
And a mother in her mourning
Remembers Greece.

Oh tell me how human affairs
Are to be measured.
Are they gauged by the wealth
Of ports, the price of alliances?
Or the torch of hope,
Extinguished daily,
That people not be divided
Into better and worse?
Hence silence. And do not say
That mighty powers are battling,
For a handful of ash will
Answer you from Grecian urns.
Which is exactly why
One remembers that land.
Our common wealth began there.

—WASHINGTON, DC, 1947

BIRTH

For the first time he sees light.
The world is garish light.
He doesn't know these are shrieks
Of garish birds.
Their hearts beat quickly
Under enormous leaves.
He doesn't know birds live
In another time than man.
He doesn't know a tree lives
In another time than birds
And will grow slowly
Upward in a gray column
Thinking with its roots
Of the silver of underworld kingdoms.

The last of the tribe, he comes
After great magic dances.
After the dance of the Antelope,
After the dance of the Winged Snakes
Under an eternally blue sky
In a valley of brick-red mountains.

He comes after spotted thongs
On a shield with a monster's face,
After deities who send down
Dreams by their painted eyelid,
After the rust of carved ships
Which the wind has forgotten.

He comes, after grating of swords
And voice of battle horns,
After the weird mass shriek
In the dust of shattered brick
After the flutter of fans
Over a joke of warm teacups,
After swan lake dances,
And after a steam engine.

Wherever he steps, there always
Endures traced in sand
A large-toed footprint
Which clamors to be tried out
By his childish foot arriving
Out of the virgin forests.

Wherever he goes, he always
Will find on things of the earth
A warm luster furbished
By a human hand.
This will never leave him,
It will stay with him always,
A presence close as breath,
His only wealth.

—WASHINGTON, DC, 1947

A FAMILY

On a sultry morning, Mother
Wears only her light-brown breast,
Father is soaping his cheeks
Under an iridescent light.
Is it not strange, they say,
That the currents of our bodies
Are unable to impart
Any of the things we have seen?
Memory resides in us only,
Our dreams have their anchor
In the burning ember, deep,
By the chambers of the sea.
For the child our tale is alien
As the words of Josephus Flavius,
Or Gibbon's *Decline and Fall*
Of the Roman Empire.

Yet already we see him walking
Between the broken columns
And dressing building stones
For his one-room house.
The vineyard has grown wild,
Water hens are calling
And books with gilded backs
Serve as stands for milk.
Oh, could but our hearts
Construct a star
Stationed above his house
When he will sit on the threshold
And, from under the burdocks
Tall as if they were pines,
Through thick green rafters,
Will glance at the inhabited
Classical sky.

—WASHINGTON, DC, 1947

OCEAN

A gentle tongue lapping
Small chubby knees,
Envoys bringing salt
From a billion-year-old abyss.
Here are violet thistles,
Peached suns of jellyfish,
Here with airplane fins
And skin of graters, sharks
Visit the museum of death
Under water towers of crystal.
A dolphin shows from a wave
The face of a black boy,
In the liquid cities of the desert
Graze leviathans.

  —WASHINGTON, DC, 1947

DAY AND NIGHT

1

White as the clay of the battlefield
Where my friend fell, clutching at dry grasses,
Is the sand that erases the memory of feet,
And the white froth and glassy sheen
Of the surf reaches to my knees
And the sun, warming my shoulders,
Throws long shadows on the breaking wave:

And life was good, who could deny it?

A surge from the depths, met by the raised
Breasts of the women, broke into a spray
Of luminous dust where the surface of the water
Reflected the wings of a low-flying pelican,
And so, having been given the twentieth-century gift
Of public nakedness, we took each other
By the hand and dove into the thundering surf
Or, having abandoned a sand castle,
Sidled into the heave of a glistening wave:

And life was good, who could deny it?

2

The table set, a warm glow emanated
From the bright earth like a sheaf of flowers.
It was as if we were in a leafy arbor.
And a red bird, in flickering glimpses,
Passed over the tree and returned.
The sound of the ocean lay next to us like a dog.

While we were raising glasses to our mouths,
Someone suddenly shouted, and I glanced up.
There passed by our table in a compact line
Creatures transformed by death into insects.

Karol, Józef, Ludwik, and Antoni proceeded
At a caterpillar's pace, in a circular motion.
Death had given them a different earth,
Concerned with matters about which
Only they knew—raising brittle tents
Among the leaves perhaps, masticating
The juices of osmosis with powerful jaws,
Gnawing rotten wood with the saws of their teeth.
And they passed. Disappeared into the grass, ceremoniously.

3

I weighed her slight fruits in my hand.
And plaited her heavy hair on the bedding
In the green gallery of the hot world.
And night was over us, as night will be
When, in the navy-blue emptiness, a star
Whitens so brightly it is almost winged.

And it was so quiet that we could hear
How, far above us, the pale silver ball
Turned slowly, playing its slow music,
Similar to bas-reliefs in a Mexican house
Of seas on the shield of the sun,
Unreachable and akin to earth.

At bottom where the little lamps of insects glow,
A fly has begun to buzz and kept buzzing,
Caught in a net forged by spiderwebs.
Poor fly, with a half-childish face,
Envious that one of us did not remain
At the long-forgotten barricade.

—WASHINGTON, DC, 1947

REFLECTIONS

An ant trampled, and above it clouds.
A trampled ant and above it a column of azure sky.
And in the distance, marking its blue steps,
The Vistula or the Dnieper on its bed of granite.

This is the image reflected in the water:

A city ruined, and above it clouds.
A ruined city and above it a column of azure sky.
And in the distance, stepping over blue thresholds,
The remains of History or the Spring of myth.

A dead field mouse, and beetle gravediggers.
On the footpath, running, a seven-year-old joy.
In the garden a rainbow-colored ball and laughing faces
And the yellow luster of May or April.

This is the image reflected in the water:

A defeated tribe, armored gravediggers.
Along the road, running, a millennial joy,
A field of cornflowers blooming after the fire,
And the silence is blue, everyday, normal.

This is the image reflected in the water.

—WARSAW, 1942–WASHINGTON, DC, 1948

"Just what, oh poet, do you propose to save?
Can anything save the earth?
This so-called dawn of peace,
What has it given us? A few morning glories
Among the ashes. It gave hopes bile, the heart
Cunning, and I doubt it roused much pity."

So this is my subject for today:
From you it will require the discipline
Of paring down. And you must resist
Filling the blanks with theories. However
Meekly and politely. The sparest collection
Of sentences is changed when you change
The place from which you look at them:
Browsing the Icelandic sagas, you do not
Altogether give them credence.
You doubt the veracity of Hindu myths.
The knowledge of Atlantis is foreign to you,
And the totems of primitive peoples
Are not going to alter your customs.
(Anyway, let's grant them due respect,
Every day, as necessary, in tribute.)
Look this way at today's fables,
A bit askance. Although seriously.

Poor Hypatia, whom they stripped
Naked in the market square of Alexandria,
And the witches in the city of Salem
Went to their deaths (undoubtedly with great sorrow),
Scylas, executed by the Scythians
Because he offered presents to Greek gods.
And more: poisons swallowed in prisons
And the short sword fretting a wound.

If you know what happened afterward,
You're way ahead of Herodotus;
Well acquainted with the edge of night,
Settle down with Thucydides, and distil
The purple juice, until you've touched
With your finger the kernel of a style.
Then see what human footprint's in the legend.

Similarly, reach into our fogged-over days,
Enveloped in style as in a cocoon,
And pluck at thread after thread,
Until the fragile yarn unravels,
And there appears, slowly, at bottom,
The inviolable chrysalis of events.
Then roll up the yarn. And act—
Until your days are over—
In full knowledge that only in this way
Can you track that scalding star of transformations.

Method, however, won't suffice
Until humankind grows older, and
With, let's call it, musical knowledge
Arrives at some great tangent,
That is to say, a wisdom as flexible,
As masterly homo sapiens himself.

Meanwhile, everyone thirsts for a faith,
Asks to be shown the counselling center,
Shouts: it is so; thus saith the prophet.
They cite him *expressis verbis*,
Threaten apostates with a dark cell.
They sing a song of war in the press,
Broadcast fiery calls to arms
Under the banner of words without definition,
And they put a volume of the encyclopedia
In the pot as if they were going to eat it.

Our epoch, that is to say, our demise,
That is to say, *Die* gigantic *Liquidation*—
I am unable to say how long it will last,
What sorts of scoundrels we shall hear from—
Value it (albeit with slight reservations),
For through it the world is changing.

The life of a gravedigger is jolly.
He buries systems, faiths, schools,
He tamps the earth down smoothly over them
With a quill, a revolver, or a shovel,
Full of hope that with the coming of spring
A marvelous flower will arise in this place.
But there ain't no spring. It's always December.
Let's not, however, dispel illusions.

Today I invite you onto the ark,
Which will bear us across the rapid stream
Of time and onto new shores.
You land in a sunken forest,
The fogs burn off, a rainbow overhead,
And a dove offers you a green leaf.
In a hundred, or perhaps in two hundred years,
Somewhere in Taormina, perhaps in Trieste,
In France (the China of Europe),
Or where the graves of capitals lie today,
A tiny center of learning will shine
And give the password to a new fatherland.
Look how the perspective has changed:
What once seemed great to us
Is no longer called great.
The chronicles are now so many empty pages.
Those who make history today
Will be committed to the sod.
A grandson of the barbarians

Sits there in the sun, reading pensively.
The ancient laurels burn on his forehead.
He is thinking of those about whom
Ballads are being sung again, who preserved
The treasure and bore it across the darkness.

It is not my intent, however,
To surround the future with empty magic.
What's the use of an illusion of the future
If it blasphemes against our quotidian days
And does not share our confidence
Equally among our fellow citizens.
You live here, now. *Hic et nunc.*
You have one life, one point.
Whatever you manage to accomplish will remain
(No matter what anybody else thinks.)
A new convention is already taking shape.
Don't say: the convention of the long knives.
I have no doubt it will be very bad,
But it was not I who invented it.
You may accuse, if you like,
The golden ingots in Venetian banks,
Elizabeth, Luther, the end of the Armada,
The balls in Versailles, military reviews,
The Tartars, because they invaded us,
The Hundred Years' War—and so on.
Even if you come to envy dogs and birds,
You have to accept the convention as it is.
Simply as an event on our revolving stage—
And you float on this social fact
Like a nut in a cataract of the Nile.

You are not, however, so helpless,
And even if you were a stone in a field,
An avalanche changes its course

Depending on the stones it rolls over.
And as someone else used to say,
You have the power. Influence the course
Of the avalanche. Moderate its wildness
And cruelty. This too requires courage,
And though the modern state
Thunders against Samaritan service,
We have seen too many crimes
For us to be able to renounce the good,
To say—Blood is cheap today—
And to be able to sit down to breakfast calmly.

Or, seeing the necessity of spoken nonsense,

To accept it as our daily bread.
And so remember: in a difficult moment,
You must be the ambassador of dreams,
Of those sleepy dreams from the depths of darkness
That have the chubby face of the Baroque,
Or a gentle Etruscan joke in the eyelids
Like the scales of a pinecone.
Three thousand years weave themselves
Into your sleep and tell of the past,
And your political subterfuges
Are accompanied by a Rabelaisian guffaw.

I know what sort of temptation awaits us:
The new march sets off jauntily,
The posthumous hiccup of Heidelberg,
The solace of despairing intellectuals.
In spite of all, the *Ding an Sich*
Still lingers on in them.
So, lost amidst the chaos,
They have grasped at the new manner,

And, wishing to have something that lasts,
They found this: *Être pour Soi.*
I would gladly give them the palm of glory,
But those things are not to be had,
Since no one from that convention (or formation)
Is likely to get off the train at some station
To amuse himself pleasantly
With a net for catching *Être* or butterflies.
Raising children, making laws,
A person stands before the Almighty,
Makes eternity in the action of a moment,
And the Sartrean contradiction is alien to him.
(It is better to live without Fear and Trembling
Than to fall into the trap of ontology.)

I do not speak here of the entire aura
In which Paris just now wallows.
Once again on Boulevard Saint-Michel—
It's all myth and Georges Sorel,
And Bergson again, *élan vital.*
It is truly painful, and a pity.
Worse: on the lovely breasts of young girls—
A volume of Jaspers bound in leather.
You just can't kill this German stuff—
Just take the example of Heidegger.

Don't think, because of what I said at the beginning,
That I do not condemn these bits of nonsense.
My skepticism encompasses
A rush to method, with a joke for content,
While these irrational ones
See the world in the form of a great tub,
Where everyone rummages in the magma
And chooses what he will.

Please don't draw any conclusions,
Schoolboy style, from my words.
As if to throw Sartre under the cupboard
And stage a little auto-da-fé;
On the contrary, in my theory
Heresy strides in great glory.
For the salt of an epoch is in heresy,
Especially when the writers are not too shabby.[1]

In any case, do not rely much on foreigners.
Here at home, Witkiewicz is an interesting case.
A rapacious mind. Not to read
His books is almost a duty.
In the next hundred years, I suppose,
No one will publish his works in Poland,
And the milieu he came out of
Will have become quite incomprehensible,
Not even the best expert will have a clue
What sort of poison was in him.

---

1   I am of the opinion, however,
That there could be persecutions,
And I wish to warn my countrymen
At the outset with the following tale.
A misadventure occurred in Kraków:
Someone brought chocolates to a young lady,
And there on the bed, en passant,
He found a copy of *L'Être et Néant*.
I see a crowd of lady existentialists,
Naked, each quivering like a leaf,
Dragged out onto St. Mary's Square,
Scoffed at and lashed with switches.
And being given, in spite of civil liberties,
Fifty-five years hard labor.
I don't know whether Sartre's old book
Was worth such punishment
And although this is a joke, the thing is possible.
This is what happens to existentialists.

My poem should be a refuge against despair,
Precisely the sort that Witkacy had,
When, accurately seeing a part of the truth,
He himself fell through his own trapdoor,
And in that September full of sorrow,
With a strong dose of barbital,
Considered death such a thing of honor
That what he began he finished with a straight razor.
Balzac is the antidote for him:
Everything that keeps us on a short leash
And by expanding the earthly edifice,
Awakens the passion for human affairs.

Enough about books. It is people who are important.
It takes quite an imagination
To judge them accurately today,
Walking in prudence, as if in a helmet.
I must seriously warn you:
It is easier than you think to lose your soul
Through unsuitable company,
For you are a sponge: you absorb everything.
The principle must be strict:
Let nothing escape examination;
Your vision must be like an X-ray.
(The picture won't always be pretty.)
Better you seem cold and dry
Than that the tropical moss of unwashed souls,
The stalactites of the terrible night,
Should grow over you.
Judge people by my method, I tell you:
It is most strictly aristocratic.

Beware madmen. They are nice enough
As long as they are confined to institutions,
Or kept in an ordinary stable.

Today there are competent madmen.
And each, my child, waves
His wand from on high.
Truly, a madman on the loose
Is the greatest disaster in nature.

This is no time for sneering, for the age
Has bred a peculiar type of schizophrenia.
If I believe in a *finis terrae*,
It is not because the means are infinite—
And that they have made the Bomb Atomic—
But because there has appeared the catatonic
As a certain social type,
And he is to tackle the challenge of progress.
Hence the psychological significance
Of this atomic business.
Babel has laid the last brick
Of two parallel disasters.

For schizophrenia is a splitting of the being
In two, into flower and root,
The sense that *it isn't I but someone else*
Performing these deeds of mine.
So that to break someone's neck is a trifle,
Then to read the *Divine Comedy*,
Or to applaud an old quartet,
Or discuss the avant-garde.
On a lesser scale, this is a daily thing.
Someone says: evil is nameless,
And we are merely its instruments.
He's right. And he rushes to his doom.

This phenomenon, as it appears to us,
Results from the pressure of avalanches
On soil where the centuries had laid down
A firmly settled ethical foundation.

If I may be permitted once again
The parable of the parabola:
This different splitting of the atom
Has come to aid the ideas of the physicists.

How to recognize them? The shape of the eyelids
Is not that of a normal human being,
And the dull insect gleam in their eyes—
That is what most often betrays them.
It's a look that's not foreign to me.
I've already seen it in Gestapo officers,
Also in Hieronymus Bosch,
Where demons on infernal couches
Stick pitchforks into the damned.
It's a familiar sight, though repellent.
In any case, they know how to maintain a façade,
So take this as a kind of approximation.

Besides this, do not judge too rashly,
For there are various degrees of insanity,
And willy, or perhaps nilly,
We are all embraced in its thrall.
This is how the unpleasant truth is revealed:
Today, insanity is the cost of action,
And probably only a hermit,
Reading Augustine in his tower,
Thinks he will be able to escape it.
The merit of this is dubious.
However, think what you wish:
I will only remind you here
That the devil, as I know from my reading,
Is *séparé de lui-même.*

Avoid those who, in their own company,
Playing the political horses,
While the fire crackles in the hearth,

Shout: the people, and whisper: dregs,
Shout: the nation, and whisper: crap.
I think they act very badly,
Because they're drunk on appearances,
They themselves are only meteors,
And long years will await them under the earth,
And much water will flow in the Vistula
Before anyone will give a peep about them.

And I advise you, by all means,
Not to keep company with those
Who are blind as moles
In a garish and muscular age.
They would like to live in their own parish,
To sit in gardens of mallow and sage,
And sometimes to see in the amaranths
The army riding along a Polish road.
They would like spinning wheels to whir
To the beat of an ur-Polish stanza.
And to live here in an idyll
(If only as on the Persian Gulf).
Thus with a Sarmatian relish
Do they inhabit a land of muddy emotions,
Which is pretty much a swamp:
Take its depth, and it pulls you in deeper.

Anyway, supported by intuition
And a healthy dose of contempt,
You will find your way
Better than I can show you.
And since it is decidedly unbecoming
To cast a stone at one's neighbor,
I have good and proper reason
Not to mention the artists.
Wishing, however, to offer you a sign,

I will utter an enigmatic word:
Every flaw of personality
Is multiplied a hundredfold in art.
If verse and prose wither,
Don't seek external reasons. Look into the crux of the matter.
He who has found sad cynicism to his taste
Is not going to evade his fate.
Even lions don't put on a brave face
When they find themselves in a losing game.

You have probably already noticed:
I stress your way of life.
Since this is where you spend your time,
So let's speak of alcohol.

Poland bows down in difficult times,
With little jokes and anecdotes,
Before the idol of vodka and kielbasa,
Nostalgic for the mead of the old nobility.
And before tears, and after tears,
It reels in ur-Slavonic fashion,
And, toting up its poverty in hiccups,
Finds a multitude of reasons for boasting.

The phenomenon of vodka is interesting,
It would be worth a dissertation.
Of all drinks, vodka alone
Is akin to the fumes of extermination.
In it you can see the shimmer of burning cities,
Through its thin glass the convicts go.
And when the houses hiss at night
And the fire is a pupil in the eye of the windows,
The brothers Karamazov, with glum faces,
Have sat down to a liter.
As the smell of formic acid rising from an antheap

Grows stronger in the summer heat,
So the odor from this misfortunate land
Gives a signal to travelers coming from afar:
"The civilization of blood and tears,
La civilisation des punaises."
And although it will seem strange to you
That I waste my time and energy
Making verse about this (noncompulsory) evil,
The question, though not primary, matters.

Farewell. Let us pass from hand to hand
The common gift of modest wisdom.
As you see, I do not have a prescription,
I do not belong to any sect,
And the rescue is in you alone.
Perhaps it is simply health
Of mind, a balanced heart.
For at times a simple remedy helps,
As when a doctor, weary
With answering gibberish
And beaten down with charlatanism,
Recommends a steak, chicken soup, milk.
This is your world on a sword edge:
The wind picks up, and stirs little eddies
Of dried leaves in the grass;
Pigeons soar over the rooftops.
A dog barks, a child runs by,
Somebody signals someone with a handkerchief.
This is your world. It is on the line.
The politicians have already lost the game,
Their apparent triumphs
Are just so much summer lightning,
Although none of them will ever lose
Trust in the power of indoctrination,

Which delivers them hordes of followers.
But the social test tubes are more complicated.
Elements swim in them like undiscovered stars.
A newly added element now and then
Shatters the walls of the laboratory.
And what now flows down
Becomes the century's liquor.
The result is entirely unpredictable.
Let's assume the result will be good.
If you have penetrating vision,
You see things marvelous to others,
Just as ultraviolet light
Shows us a new image;
And coursing through sharp turns of matter,
Reveals to us alien components
And pigments in common objects:
This is usually worthy of examination.
For now, I give you no hope,
Do not wait in vain for the Treuga Dei,
For you will not escape by some magic gate
The life that has been given you.
Let us go in peace, we simple people.
I need to say this with some starkness:
Before us lies

"The Heart of Darkness."

—WASHINGTON, DC, 1947

1948, WASHINGTON, DC

SUMMER MOVIES IN CENTRAL PARK
For Juliusz Kronski in Paris

In the dim light on the trampled grasses
Girls lie still with soldiers in their arms.
Until the image alters: dark glance
Of a shoulder, an unbuttoned blouse.

Trees spring from the ancient bedrock
And the sprays of leaves fall like chords.
When nature becomes a theater,
The silvery machinery of the skyline shifts.

The summits of the abstract city quiver
Under murky rainbows in the humid air.
Honeycombs of metal, or stalactites,
Divide the distance into sheer domains.

. . .

I remember a field where the radiance
Of the burning city colors the dry wormwood
And crickets play, red from the glow,
Through which an army of smoke marches.

The water rushing along the road flutters
The dress on the corpse of a woman,
As the city descends long days and nights
Into legend, which won't compensate for its disasters.

This memory contains a warning for those
Who spend their nights on soft couches:
An errant fire will often burn right through
The rosy stains on bedsheets.

Whoever enters the human microcosmos
Where marvels are performed should know
That it delivers, serenely, on a daily basis,
The retributions of a malignant fate.

They don't hear this. As if the fresh earth
Had brought forth the first palm after the flood,
Trembling, they enter the quiet groves of sex
and simply give themselves to each other.

And yet even here, in the middle of Manhattan,
I could see how, at a warning sound,
Their faces blanch in the glare of the screen
And sudden fright weakens their legs.

Here, in the line of cars along 5th Avenue,
I see how the ambassador's limousine glides
Past the white masts on which various flags
Of fictitious color sway in a mild breeze.

The poor envoys. Their labors are great,
As they, eyes asquint, compose a holy covenant
With duplicitous ink, or the pact
Between the Athenians and the Lacedemonians.

And what sort of power was granted to us,
Juliusz, when we foresaw the fate
Of our native realm, which was to be brought
Under the militarized feet of foreign powers.

We had barely mourned in our secret hearts
That Europe, mothers of arts and sciences
With its old wisdom and bloody cobblestones,
As we placed it on the scales opposite the new faith.

Looking calmly at force, we know that the ones
Who want to rule the world will pass away
And we know that it isn't always necessary
To live by the knife and the submachine gun.

We know that the ingenuity of our weapons
Is disastrous, that the whirlwind shreds banners,
And that the heirs to the glory of the Greek name
(But glory, our heritage from Greece)
Will last as long as humankind lasts.

And that this age of darkness will pass the way winters
Pass when strong sap rises under the brittle bark.
The smile of the Sophists, as in papal Rome,
Will knock the pen from the hand of the Inquisitors.

Just as once upon a time books were brought
From Constantinople to the northern lands,
The voices of wise men in the wild lands
Will become a source of creative power.

It is this honor, Juliusz, that is granted us:
To resurrect new forms, forged of gold.
In spite of the leisurely pace of change,
To mix valiant drinks for the future.

Greet the Parisian streets for me, please,
And the fountain in the Luxembourg Gardens.
Likewise the Seine where, to this day, I can see
The Cathedral's arches and the sleeping boats.

I don't know whether Montaigne's monument
Still stands, whose white marble lips
A girl, as a joke, has painted blush red,
And run off, lowering her head in laughter.

There are, according to the Greek philosophers,
Seven stages to the journey. We may not be familiar
With them all, so let this wandering road
Through the ashes of war be your chosen path.

And receive as a gift an afternoon's description
Of this excessively proud land
And with it my hope that books will preserve
This little drawing of Central Park.

—WASHINGTON, DC, 1948

UNTITLED

The sad little birds of the eternal spring
In steep, cold San Francisco.
Joy here has a doleful taste,
Although it is dressed in Paris style.

The seals lie barking on rocks
Washed by the ocean waves.
Blues, whites of the hills above the bay.
(Wanda favors Economic Planning)

And, well, the people here as usual:
Energetic and silly.
One speaks in these banalities
When actually the heart bleeds.

And remember the terrible fish?
One looked like a Javanese dancer
And also recalled the Habim—
Something probably improbable.

Another we named Odetta, as in Proust:
A patterned suit, cut in at the waist
And the pink lips of the haut bourgeois.
Crude, I know. I called it *Odettynska.*

Recall, too, the bitter scent
Of rubbed eucalyptus.
Take that back to Poland with you.
Tell them what sort of fare they eat here.

     —SAN FRANCISCO, JUNE 6, 1948

THE PEOPLE'S GRAPHIC WORKSHOP

(*El Taller de Gráfica Popular*)

I

The sun flows over the mountains, the valleys,
And the din of hammers reverberates, women's voices,
    the rustling of bare feet on the earth.
Smoke wafts over the cornfields and the blue slopes of volcanos,
The sparks of a smithy fly over the waters of the deep.

For many days, many years, and many centuries
An Indian walked at daybreak, crumbling in his fingers a clod of
    yellow soil,
Girls bore pots on their heads along the winding paths,
And in the evening on the village square the drum boomed and
    the viol squeaked.

Songs and a gathering of stories,
Whose words the old women repeated from memory:
The iron glove of Cortez's knights,
The white and gold of the cupolas of churches on the heights,
The clip-clop of the rider in a kaftan of black velvet,
The saddle studded with rubies and the silver spurs.
The bustle of the markets, years of hunger,
Suppliant processions in the dust in a time of drought,
And the signs by which one recognizes the way
To the ruins of the temple of the sun in the tangle of the forests.

II

Man's heart desires,
Faust's dream is the light of his blood:
To stop over a great, teeming, joyous valley,
To listen to songs sung at the hour of wise labors,
And to drink the jug of brotherhood with the fortunate.
Man's thought pushes up from the arable soil
Of daily matters, from fragile circumstances,
In a cold hour, at the edge of night.
Juanita stepped upon a thorn, and cries.
A wife combs black hair, and the russet tips of her breasts wobble,
Little Jose tinkles in the middle of the room and eyes this with
    careful wonderment,
Chewing on a straw, a man comprehends in thought both
    heaven and earth,
And he imagines many rooms, and in each
There sits a person, deep in thought, chewing on a straw.
Later, in the pink twilight,
The great book lies open, and with a rough finger a man
Slowly, slowly follows and assembles the letters.

III

Intentions arise from fragile circumstances,
The penetrating smell of sweat and urine, of sickness,
The lack of money for flour and olive oil,
Torn pants, the worn soles of sandals
Accompany them or lead them.
Three rented rooms in a moldy courtyard
That friends called The People's Graphic Workshop.
And they set up a handpress of the sort on which
The Paris Commune had supposedly printed its leaflets.

To express the sounds of human mouths with a stylus:
Cries and lamentations,
A lover's whisper, a wedding song,
The breath of the weary, a curse,
The call to arms and a battle cry.
To express the memory of the people with a stylus,
Old beliefs, conquests
And quotidian days, and hope.
That was the intent. This happened
In nineteen thirty-eight.

IV

Those who cut sugarcane,
Those who work in salt mines,
Those who yoke oxen to the plow,
Pitmen surfacing from the tunnel of a mine,
Lumberjacks sawing logs in a bay,
The loading of vegetables onto narrow skiffs,
The plaiting of hats from fibers of bekal,
The husking of corn, canteens,
Women preparing tesgüino,
Musicians with double basses, great drums,
The silence of barges floating on Rio Palizada,
Village traders and barbers,
Markets, processions, carousels.

And bandoleers crossed on the chests of those whom Zapata led,
And standards over the heads of the crowd: Peace, Land,
    and Bread,
And the dances of the maliciously smiling skeletons
Against the background of pimps of New York goods,
And drawings according to the frescos painted twelve hundred
    years ago,
And life in Morelia, Huichol, on the Yucatán.

The chisel of artists gave a particular tone
To each man, each child, and each woman.
In millions of faces and hands no two alike.
A body was a body, blood was blood.
And more powerful than the letters of the big books,
From fragile circumstances and from doubt
Arose the work
Of the People's Graphic Workshop.

V

Endless days,
Under the sun sacrificial knives, the rustle of bare feet, cuirasses
    of Cortez in the dust of volcanic earth.
The convening of people under the crooked lightning flash of a
    dagger in the fields,
New settings-out in the circle of death and nuptials.
Endless days,
Those that were, and those that will be.
In the warm interior of a frail throat, in the tremor that runs
Through hardworking fingers, a voice began.
The huge fiddles of the Mexican valleys
Resounded with it and amplified it.
Until, under snowy moons and the lashing of monsoons,
It made itself heard and ran the planet round.

    —WASHINGTON, DC, 1948

A CONCERT

Who are those dwarves with faces of forest bark
Extracted from caves under the roots of trees,
Resting their grasshopper legs on the bank
And leaning forward in rows, while the left hand
Wrests rapture from the instrument's box,
And the right joins an army of glittering bows?

From the whispers of mice in the dry leaves of winter,
From a tree hollow full of excrements and familiar squeaks,
Men come together and perform a thing that doesn't exist
Under the shell of the sky or in the grottos of the sea.
Chased by this sound plains open up
And the voice of a female singer is the source of the radiance
When a low spark sets the grass on fire.

Her long legs, swathed in the thick fabric of her gown,
Press her toes, gold-sandaled, to the stage.
Inside her warm mouth the rondure of her voice
Is transformed into a metal keyboard.
Marble columns parade before her sight
Until a shiver of triumph loosens her hands:
A flock of bravos, coves of silence.

From the yellow clay under the darkness of foundations,
Bones in dress from the last days of the Empire
Watch the spectacle through glass floors.
They see the dwarves, legs astraddle, instruments in their hands,
Double basses, golden feet, and the singer—
That is, the succulent line of her legs.

—WASHINGTON, DC, 1948

THE JOURNEY

In pink fingers of magnolia,
In the downy softness of May,
In the leap from branch to branch
Of a bird, pure colored, a cardinal,
Between breasts of calm rivers
Lies this city
Into which I ride with a bouquet of stiff roses
On my knees, like the jack of hearts,
Shouting for joy of spring
And the shortness of life.

Waves of scent, a song,
Wet armfuls of purple flowers
Shaken off by a black hand,
Tunnels of neon lights,
The green, and a song again,
Bridges over the birds' realms,
Streetlights—teddy bears' eyes
Made of rubies.

Afternoon whiskers,
Thorny braids of black girls,
Cool drinks, shadowy glasses
At lips painted in the shape of a heart,
Mannequins with thighs in silk,
Constantly combed cemeteries
Recede into night, rocket-like,
Into a bursting night
Tralala
Tralali
Into oblivion.

    —WASHINGTON, DC, 1948

63

THE PALACE OF MY MUSES

Alas, a make-believe land
Of cactus shadow,
A hirsute evening star,
The imitator of silence.
Alas, disguised grasshoppers
With their shells on the staffs of pilgrims,
Alas, through the wall you hear
The screeching of wound-up nightingales.

Alas, one rose leaf,
The bum of a pretty girl—
Night will submerge everything in the trash can.
Was it my, was it my fault?

Alas, a droplet of rum—
The delicate hours fade out,
Like a flea in the deluge of the night,
Was it my fault, or perhaps not my fault?

O Terpsichore, o Euterpe,
I loved you so, so much!
On the winds of clumsy suffering
I built a hummingbird house.

Was it because I was faithful
That I brought you flowers, seashells?
I collected pearls in a bucket
Absorbed by that sort of craft?

Alas the grasshoppers remove
Their bizarre disguise,
The springs of the nightingales have broken
And they hang dead on the wall,
The electrical wiring of the star
Has been cut, and the cacti, that is
The monuments, show us their heels.
Alas, the wind has carried the feathers away.
It's been extinguished, a make-believe land.

—WASHINGTON, DC, 1948

TO TADEUSZ RÓŻEWICZ, POET

All the instruments agree in joy
When a poet enters the garden of the earth.
Four hundred azure rivers labored
At his birth, and the silkworm
Spun for him its shimmering nests.
The corsair wing of the midge, the snout of the butterfly
Were formed with him in mind.
And the many-storied edifice of the lupine flower
Brightened night for him at the edge of a field.
In this way all the instruments, shut up
In cases and pitchers of greenery,
Wait for him to touch them and sing out.

Praise to the corner of the earth that brings forth a poet!
Tidings of this flow on the near-shore waters
Where, sleeping on the surface, fogs and seagulls float
And, further out, where ships rise and fall.
The tidings flow under the mountains of the moon.
And the moonlight shows the poet at his desk
In a cold room in a little-known town
Where the clock in the tower is striking the hour.

His home is in the pine needle, the cry of the roe deer,
In the explosion of stars, and the inside of the human hand.
Clocks do not measure his song. The echo,
The ancientness of the sea, as in the middle of a shell,
Is never silenced. The poet endures. And the whisper
Of his voice is great and gives comfort to people.
Happy the nation that has a poet.
In his toils they do not walk in silence.

Only rhetoricians do not like the poet.
Sitting on chairs of glass, they unfurl
The long scrolls, the grants of nobility.
All around them the laughter of the poet
And his life has no limit.

The rhetors are wrathful. They know their chairs will break,
That in the place where they sit, not a blade of grass
Will grow. Even ants will bypass
The circle of burnt sulfur, the barren red dust.

—WASHINGTON, DC, 1948

TO ALBERT EINSTEIN (FRAGMENTS)

In a blue tricot shirt and with the face
Of a clockmaker from the Jewish neighborhood in Warsaw,
With a pipe and a white mane, smiling sadly,
Allow me, gracious old man, to offer you a poem.
To use poetry in such a fashion brings me joy.
The need to adore is strong. A girl
Hangs a picture of her favorite movie star on the wall.
For me, I admit, life would not have essence
If I were not able to admire. I hide in my heart
Unspoken words constantly. I regret being so little able
To help people value the great beauty of the world.
Everything interested me. The names of trees and plants,
The rise of species, Darwin's journeys,
Polynesian myths, the mating dress of birds,
Half-obliterated sculptures in forgotten lands.
The microscopes in cold laboratories enticed me,
I learned several languages, wishing to read
About the fifth century in Rome, Greece, Alexandria,
And about the sixteenth century in maritime Europe,
Critical epochs, and similar to mine which arose for me,
A child, in the ashes of the first World War,
The thunder of cannons, the bellowing of cattle
Driven on roads over which our refugee cart
Was driven in the dust. If I turn to you today,
It is not only because, forged from marble,
Your bust stands where Newton and Copernicus
Stand in our memory. Not that you succeeded
In placing an equal sign between gravity
And electricity. There is something greater in you:
Faith in the light of reason, invincible concern
For our human species, for what it can be
And also for what it can, despicably, squander.

Not the cold of a neutral explorer of Nature,
But the warmth, the anxiety of genuine goodness.
I'm ashamed to speak it out loud. The matter
That it is so difficult to name, the matter of hope,
Chafes. I have seen people transformed into beasts
Or locked in the prison house of learned illusions.
I am writing this in the capital of the United States.
It's summer, the birds are making a racket along the avenues.
Bright-colored cars speed by. People on the greens
Play ball, play golf, grill hot dogs on the fire grates
In the park. The radios on the motorcycles
Bleat about spies, about fugitive criminals,
War, Communists, and about new weapons.
This New Jerusalem of the old Puritans,
Their dream realized however much the wrong way,
Is for me an empty stage set, and a burden,
As if I wished to cry out in my sleep, and can't.

. . .

I have, however, learned to say no. This is,
Of old, the privilege afforded to poets,
That wages, weddings, baptisms, and funerals
Are not matter for us. A brilliance, perhaps,
A play of lights over vast, black waters. As if
We walked past a glassed-in garden, seeing,
With regret, more than is allowed.
Are we in fact the enemies of the species,
Who wish to change human beings by force
Into angels of pure intellect, to tear from the depths
A hated spark of Promethean torture.

    —WASHINGTON, DC, 1948–49

1949, WASHINGTON, DC

MY MOTHER'S GRAVE

1

A small silver globe in motion and planets
Circulating in the orbits of electrons
Around the sun of the atom. But for us
There always exists one point on the earth
That returns in the senselessness
Of dreams, when headless mannequins
With wooden necks lead the dance
Or dogs jump on legs of carved wood.
Between memory, which troubles us,
Because it says there is no conquering the past,
And oblivion, which is an insult
To our notions of our own goodness,
We live unstably, while in a rush
Like flies in the light of incessant lamps,
Electron passes electron in the void.

2

Oh, how the sea booms these fall nights
At the mouth of the Vistula. Thunder fills
The flat bottomlands under the ranks of willows
And a north wind combs the dry grasses,
Rattles the tall weeds, and showers glass
From the broken windows of the dead church.
Long shields of thick metal,
Washed with heavy drops of rain,
Return eroded names to the clouds
Near the place where the earth and the remains
Of her who bore me are joined
To eternal solitude, the cries of migratory birds,
And the dull, incessant respiration of the sea.

3

It was pure daybreak over the water, mother.
A rosy tint on the white breast of a bird
And the tranquil rays of the early sun
And mist rising from the dark bullrushes.
Until in a sudden pall dark clouds covered the sun
And stinging tears filled our eyes. Why
is it, mother, that neither a morning nor a flower
Nor the dusky apple on its rough bough
Lasts longer than the blink of an eye?
Why does the butterfly's wing open for a flight
Measured by the grains in an hourglass?
And why, mother, do you yourself cease to be
The beautiful girl I was in love with?
Is there no paint, gold or transparent,
With which to dye the fresh rose:
No way to keep them forever and ever,
The flowers and mornings, trees and butterflies?
I have been giving my life to this question,
Wanting to be like a sheet of water,
Repeating what is reflected there just once,
Not caring whether I prolong the world
By an entire age or by a single moment.

4

And then, mother, comes maturity,
And with it the aspiration to bring
What's complicated to its simplest form,
And the desire to serve people. It is then
That great principles appear, by which collectives
Grow and perish, and one passes with regret
The window behind which, in a circle of lamplight
A family sits at the table, unaware of fate.

And tomorrow's tears enter the quiet orchards
And that small life—crumbly clay
That the iron glove crushes—
Is the material for a bloody epic.
The irrepressible momentum of rapid rivers—
Useless to stand aside wringing one's hands.
This age, set ablaze by human bodies,
Let it rather devour our dreams.

5

But among those who understand the harvest
of nations and the flight of a lightning bolt,
There are, as in the days of the prophets,
The righteous man and the loquacious man
Of unclean heart. Why, mother, would I not believe in Hell
When I have exchanged handshakes
With those who bear in their unseeing eyes
The disquiet and falseness of the condemned?
O accursed dogs, torturers of man,
Who ask with a laugh, "What is man?"
Or shout, "For man! For man!"
With a foot resting on their neighbor's throat.
O those misfortunates who don't even know
A moment of fear under the expanse of the sky
And who never admit to themselves
The knowledge they have of themselves.
It's not true, mother, that in the human species
There are neither the saved nor the damned.
And yet who will dare to say, "I am righteous,"
When cowardice breeds indifference
And indifference silence about crime
And crime only death and accusations.

6

Looking into the counterfeit ledgers,
Where they enter the falsified judgments,
Who will dare to invoke history
In order to lay claim to his deeds?
Who would devote himself to the paper laurels
That he has readied for his own statue?
Who will be satisfied to receive encouragement
Or affirmation from his own shadow,
To trust the years, until they smash him into dust?

7

Help me to create a love eternally alive
From my constant quarrel with the world.
A single link of inspiration and action,
Unknown to the productions of unthinking nature.
A thing only human, into which a swarm
Of electrons indifferently spatters its shots,
The work of a being who lives in a great house
All alone with its molds and its blemishes.
A still point that, contrary to history,
Divides what is fluid into good and evil—
Help me, mother. Strengthen in the man
What you knew as the child's ardors.
Let me not put down my burden.
Let the wind from the Vistula flow like an ocean.
You who wished to grant me the gift of life,
May you be greeted in the name of God. Amen.

—WASHINGTON, DC, 1949

A LEGEND

Nobody knows the beginning of the city.
Slushy ruts, a call at the ferry,
Resin torches, a fisherman leaning on a spear,
And fish pots and the mists of the shallows.
Then the riders with lances lead in
Half-naked prisoners and pine after pine
Falls down and with huge timbers
A castle is erected above the swift river.
Dark rafters. The whirling of dogs
Crunching bones in the gleam of shields and swords,
Shaky rushlights and whiskered shadows
Bent over pewter goblets, raucous songs.
In bedchambers, amidst spearshafts and leather bands,
Giggling of old gods. In the thicket at night
Their wild stomping and whistling. And yet already a bell
Trickled its tiny voice through the wilderness,
And the monks, raised on their stirrups,
Were turning toward the people below
Who, uncertain, faltered between their rite
And the force of the new imperious laws.

Who knows the beginning? We lived in this city
Without caring about its past. Its walls
Seemed to us eternal. Those who lived there before us
Were just a legend, undeciphered.
Our age is better, we would say. No plague, no sword
To pursue us, so why should we look back?
Let the centuries of terror sleep in the hard earth.
We tuned our instruments, evenings
In a circle of friends would bring us gladness,
Under the colorful lanterns and the green of chestnuts
Feasts were celebrated. The slenderness of our women

Pleased our eyes. Our painters used to choose
Joyous colors. Till that day arrived.

The makeup streamed down women's cheeks. Their rings
Rattled against the pavement. Eyes
Turned to the indifferent abysses of heavens
And accepted death. Foundations of ornate buildings
Burst, the dust of crushed brick
Rose with smoke to the sun, pigeons
Were falling from the sky. We propped our street fortresses
Against the rubble of our homes, till they fell,
Our fortresses, and hands, and arms. The smell of defeat,
Cadaverous, nauseating, atrocious silence
After the din of battle descended on smoldering cinders,
The autumn rain beat down and the survivors
Received upon their brows the stigma of the slave.
The enemy debased memory, ascribing to himself
Both ancient and future glory.

And then, sitting where once it had stood,
That beautiful city, sifting through our fingers
The sand of the barrens, we discovered
The sweet name of our country. It was no more
Than the sand and the rustle of the wind in wormwood.
For a country without a past is nothing, a word
That, hardly spoken, loses its meaning,
A perishable wall destroyed by flame,
An echo of animal emotions. In the sand we saw
The ashes of centuries mixed with fresh blood.
Pride then left us and we rendered homage
To men and women who once lived and ever since
We have had our home founded in history.

—WASHINGTON, DC, 1949

TO LAURA

The moon has come out from behind the oak grove.
And my road is long.
Through a hollow of ashen ruins
I ride, for Laura awaits me.

What I say, Laura, when my head
Inclines toward your lips,
Keep it carefully in your memory.
That's how we live from now on.

At a sad, historical crossroads
Where a vampire invites you as a guest,
The precious virtue of freedom remains
And it needs to be won every day.

Thousands will put on their own shackles
And poison their hearts.
But you, you believe in me,
So try, as I try.

Take birds as a gift. Look at the stars.
Make a smile your salutation.
Just remember: each day will tell
Who of us ceases to be free.

—WASHINGTON, DC, 1949

SIEGFRIED AND ERIKA

That city, like slovenly bedclothes in the depths of night,
The dust and rubble, pursue me, Erika.
Such a meeting. The heraldic escutcheon torn down
From the gates of a Silesian manor house and trampled.
And Frau Matylda in a white ruff, against a background of
    Flemish portraits,
Died of typhus on the muddy roads.
I know only one thing: that order is inconstant.
Chaos encompasses our intentions,
Patiently awaiting its hour.
The corslet of honor and armor falls.
What remains is merely the fearful gaze
Of compliant eyes in the depths of an unshaven face,
A tattered military overcoat, pimping,
And political advice whispered to the ear
Of the new ruler: fate.
Or women: their gait so nimble.
Breasts borne so proudly, and then
From under knotted headscarves a huddled allurement
In a garden of twisted iron, a gift
To the black GIs in exchange for a pack of Camels.
Yes, I killed. Is that bad, Erika?
The road came to me with the whistling of my reins.
And the chaos was there, do you understand? Columns
Of vehicles, bundles, filth, scorching heat, a creeping fear,
A will incapable of maintaining an intention.
The deadly sparks that ran into that crowd
From under my wing were so pure!
I remained over the world, the realized.
Form on humanity, beyond complaint.
I had power over body and machine.

I reached for the future of mankind
When the borders of chaos will recede
And there will be one undisturbed line.
A building as bright as the steel of a mast.
So they accuse us? If only they might come to know
How one takes the first step in ignorance.
The banner waves, and the love of community
Drowns out petty, unmanly doubts
That tick in us, a liberal superstition.
If only the victors might come to know how quickly
one goes from the first acquiescence
To complete faith, to the final threshold.
If that day comes, it will be they shouting
Us? We are innocent! We didn't know!
Then the burden of guilt will be cast off
And our German nation will reach again
For its proper portion. Believe me, sister.

  —WASHINGTON, DC, 1949

A THOUGHT ABOUT ASIA

I see a thin man, his haunches are covered
By a skirt of dry grass. A gentle woman
With round tawny breasts. A naked child
Playing in the red dust of the road. Above them
The arms of gods and demons are writhing
In the air, the demons of the four elements
Turn their spiteful faces away. I hear sound
From the bowels of antediluvian rock, sound of a soap bubble,
Sound of the futility of human endeavor, echo
Without a cause, laugh with which
Nothing else laughs. The man rests his hand
On the woman's breast, a child is born, the family
Searches for grain in the cracked mud of the dry earth,
And the human insect withers, and the rusty legs
Of dead grasshoppers lie tangled in the dust
And a vulture describes circles in the cloudless heat.
That sound from the depths of antediluvian rocks
Mocks man and his gods and demons.
I think about things that furnish the strength
To resist the empty awareness of fruitless time.
About the white-hot wire of the heart, about decisions
Before which no one can take shelter, can hide.
I think about all the men and women
Who find ways in themselves to overcome
The laughter of the primeval rocks.

—WASHINGTON, DC, 1949

A LITTLE NEGRO GIRL PLAYING CHOPIN

If only you had seen her, Sir Frederick.
How she places her dark fingers on the keys
And diligently bends her wooly head,
How she places her slender foot on the pedal;
Comically childlike, in a well-trodden little shoe.
And when the hall suddenly grows quiet,
The primrose of tone slowly unfurls.

If only you had seen in the hall in the semidarkness,
How her teeth glitter in her open mouth,
When the grand piano bears your cares,
And how the music falls in slanting ribbons,
And how, in the hubbub of birdsong, through the
    stained glass plashes—
It was spring, in a city unknown to you by name;
If only you had seen how those tones fly,
Pull the dust motes into a column of sunlight
Over her black face, resting on her palm—
Surely you would have said it was worth it.

  —WASHINGTON, DC, 1949

HE HAS NO SIGHT

He has neither sight nor hearing nor taste
Nor smell nor touch
Who is led softly to the twentieth floor
In a soft elevator by a girl with rose-sugar nails
Who hums a frosted song.

Without vision, hearing, and without taste,
Without smell and touch,
He drops a coin into the frosted box of the radio
And a song phosphoresces.
Water in which the bacteria have been killed,
A spring filled with synthetic perfume,
Life from which death has been removed,
Sexual organs snipped from the glittering paper.

All around an empty night without color,
And aquariums where the movement of tin fish dies away,
And food drifts down, having forgotten
The secret of the work of minerals.

When a plant enters through the glass doors,
They strip it of its shadow and its stalk,
When a felled tree arrives,
They suck out its treeness with a golden needle,
And decrepit stone, sighing,
Has to shake off its stony power.

When a man walks through the glass door,
They bind his hands from behind
And smile as they touch his eyes
And smile as they touch his ears.
When he laughs, they touch his lips with a nib of nickel,
They bend his head over a retort
So that he might breathe in and be, from then on, free.

That's when the dream of huge sails begins,
Of seas where electric dolphins leap out of the waves,
Of humid forests smelling of orchids and saffron,
Of naked women with daggers in their white necks
Left under slag heaps of scrap iron
In fields where gaunt Negroes
Fan campfires with cardboard boxes.

There he lies, dreaming the dream of ancient Edens,
The dream of a vapid film tape,
The dream of little girls cut out with scissors,
He of the white belly, hands outspread.

Then they transmit an uninterrupted stream of numbers,
And they build, with tongs made of silver,
A glass cage around his red heart.

And he rises humming, and he goes serenely,
Free from the taste of water,
From the taste of bread and wine,
From love, hate, and from fear,
And he remembers the names of all things,
And he remembers that it is good to eat
And he remembers that it is good to multiply,
Having learned to pretend to himself
That joy is joy,
Delight delight.

He is led by the girl with the frosted hands,
With barrettes resembling labia in her hair
So that no one can doubt she is a woman,
And he did not mistake the names of things.
She leads him up through columns of air
In which a bird, as if encased in amber,

Abides eternally in the folding of its long wings
And where there soars from the depths of the earth
The commotion of an army of encircled minerals,
White bubbles, white eyes of swamp gasses.

He is left behind with the cries of deer,
With the throat of a dying turtledove,
With the daring head of a rattlesnake,
With a black background of rising suns.
He is left behind with the sticky torment of tropical plants,
With the white dawn of the acacia trees,
With the warmth of a beaver's hut on a winter night,
With the ironic spectacle of the electrons.

And out of fear that he doesn't feel horror,
He tosses a coin into the frosted box of the radio
For a song, for paper palm fronds,
For life without death,
For the baseness of it.

    —DETROIT, 1949

EARTH

My sweet European homeland,

A butterfly lighting on your flowers stains its wings with blood,
Blood gathers in the mouths of tulips,
Shines, starlike, inside a morning glory
And washes the grains of wheat.

Your people warm their hands
At the funeral candle of a primrose
And hear on the fields the wind howling
In the cannons ready to be fired.

You are a land where it's no shame to suffer
For one is served here a glass of bitter liquor
With lees, the poison of centuries.

On your broken evening of wet leaves,
By the waters that carry the rust
Of centurions' sunken armor,
At the foot of blasted towers,
In the shadow of their spans like aqueducts,
Under the quiet canopy of an owl's wings,

A red poppy, touched by the ice of tears.

— WASHINGTON, DC, 1949

CAROLERS

With bagpipes, fifes, and the horns of a bull
When winds from the south blow in the cold
And white leaves fly in the frosty air
Over the pastures and over the streams
With bagpipes, fifes, and the horns of a bull,

A squall sweeps down the winter hills
With a tithe of goods in a barefoot sleigh—
Fish in baskets, a moose's head,
A clutch of wild birds and lots of game,
And bagpipes, fifes, and the horns of a bull.

Knights on horseback from the forest
In their shiny Italian cuirasses
And gold chains worn for the honor of it
And swords for guarding the castle keep
With bagpipes, fifes, and the horns of a bull.

Where they quarried stone for the churchyard
They have planted an invisible marvel:
In the swirling eddies of fresh-fallen snow
The stones are angels in white vestments,
With bagpipes, fifes, and the horns of a bull.

The road they walk winds past the castle.
Down in the kitchen a taper glows.
Wheat is boiling for their dinner
And yeomen folk are preparing the mead
With bagpipes, fifes, and the horns of a bull.

Also cymbals, hey, bring them near
When we come to the hedgerows and leap
And leap to our sports, and monster about,
And sing out loud our graceful songs
With bagpipes, fifes, and the horns of a bull.

—WASHINGTON, DC, 1949

ANTIGONE

A fragment, written in 1949, which I dedicate to the memory of the workers, students and soldiers of Hungary.

ANTIGONE:

To accept what happens just as one accepts
Seasons piling pell-mell on one another,
And on our human world to cast the same
Indifference as on mute Nature's transformations?
So long as I shall breathe I shall say—*No.*
Do you hear me, Ismene? I shall say—*No.*
Nor have I any need of consolation—
Your nighttime flowers in springtime, nightingales,
Sunshine or passing clouds, familiar streams,
No, none of these. Let whatever is left
Be left to ripen, unquelled, uncontrolled.
All that is worth remembering is our pain.
See these rust-covered ruins, my Ismene?
They know it all. Death with its crow-black wings
Has masked or muffled all those years behind us
When we might have believed this land of ours
To be like any other, and our people just
Like those who live in any other land.
The curse of fate must lead to sacrifice
And sacrifice, in turn, to fate's next curse,
And when this fate fulfills itself, the time
To protect our petty lives is over.
This is no time to shed tears on ourselves.
There is no time. Let an immense catastrophe
Sweep across this entire pitiless Earth
As for those laughing now at our despair,
Let them witness their own towns razed to dust.
Creon's law! Creon's rule! Who in the world
Is Creon when our world itself is crumbling?

ISMENE:

Indeed. But Mother and Father both lie dead
As do our brothers, and no revolt of yours
Will bring them back. So why keep looking back?
An old man with a stick in a silent city
Goes rummaging in vain for fallen sons.
Old women quietly mourn amidst the dust,
Then pass on by, their wizened heads bowed down.
Yet even in bleak neighborhoods, life greens again.
Nettle and wormwood creep across the rubble.
Like a slip of paper in a fire, a butterfly
Goes fluttering at the rock edge of a precipice.
Children in ragged clothes return to school,
Lovers' hands clasp each other's. In all this,
Believe me, powerful rhythms reassert themselves.
Sobs commingle again with celebration—
Persephone returns again to earth.

ANTIGONE:

Fools alone believe they can live easy
By relegating Memory to the past.
Fools alone believe one city falling
Will bring no judgment down on other cities.

ISMENE:

Do not belittle how hard it is, Antigone,
To go on suffering, forcing lips and hearts
To silence. For each of these small victories
Is victory too. This struggle gives us hope.

ANTIGONE:

Sister, I need no hope of yours. Remember
I have seen the remains of Polynices
Beneath the steps of a destroyed Cathedral,
With tufts of light hair wafting from his skull
Like any little boy's. A crumpled handful
Of bones wrapped in a dark and rotting cloth.
The stench of a corpse. That was our own brother.
There was a time his heart beat just as strong
As yours and mine do. He knew joy, sang carefree
Songs—and knew the fear of death, since the same
Voices which call us now, called out in him
Toward bright vistas of a future life.
Yet, faithful to his word and pledge, he willingly
Made his choice to relinquish them, and die.
Twenty years old, a boy, handsome, and gentle,
He had to quell whatever plans he'd nourished,
Works hardly started, reticent, shy thoughts,
And alone, force his will to face destruction.
And this is he who now, by Creon's command,
Is branded Traitor, and his place some dark
Sand-blown corner out on the city's edge
Where wind goes whistling through his empty helmet.
Yet for the others, glory-peddlers, filchers,
Statues will be erected and young girls
Will lay out wreaths in all the broadest squares
And lights twinkle from torches on their names.
Here, though, nothing, but dark. The trembling hands
Of writers, impelled by debasing fear,
Will not stint in their praise for thieves of glory.
And so, those stripped of legend will pass down
Into the centuries' amnesia. Traitors? Heroes?

ISMENE:

By means of words, pain kindles into flame.
Who maintains silence, perhaps suffers more.

ANTIGONE:

These are not merely words, Ismene—not just words.
Creon shall never have the strength to build
His state upon our graves. Nor shall he found
Government upon sheer power of the sword.
The dead wield greater power—so great, no man
Can hide from it. Although on every side
He fences himself with countless guards and spies
Still they will find him out. The hours themselves
Await the ironic laughing dead to trample
Upon the madman who still disbelieves them.
Then, when he's called to settle his account,
An error, small at first, will trickle through
His calculations, tiny, as if from nowhere,
Then multiply and magnify a thousandfold,
And then, while treason torches towns and villages—
Enough—the flaw will ripen, swell to madness,
Crying, Blood! Blood! Too late by then for any
Red ink flowing from his hand to blot
That single error. It will be his end.
Does this wretched Creon think he'll govern us
As if ours were some land of brute barbarians,
As if each stone were not engrained with memories
Of its own tears of despair, tears of hope?

—WASHINGTON, DC, 1949

1950, WASHINGTON, DC

TO MYSELF, FOR AN ALBUM, NEW YEAR'S 1950

Tell me whether it is proper that I worry so
Over things about which others would laugh without regret.
Where they see a drop, I see an ocean.
Where they go singing, I barely proceed with hope.

If only I could do something. I have nothing but this pen.
Even for a skilled hand it's a treacherous weapon.
People will not hear me out, Nature will extinguish me.
I hear a voice. I don't know where it comes from

or to what it summons me. Am I ruled by delusions?
Wishing to think soberly, I flounder in sickness.
Do I take for true shapes what are only shadows?
Not helping people, harming only myself?

But if I disdain this hidden strength?
It is a lie that has befallen all poets.

. . .

The heart's pride, you say, deserves to be condemned.
It's in the power of experiment that human adaptability lies.
It's interesting, after all, to see how a man changes,
Contradicts himself and manages not to die of revulsion.

When you are already in Hell, be the devil who pushes
Into the cauldron the sweet little soul squealing mawkishly.
You will be blessed by both Piast and Rzepicha.
Is it better to be the devil than the sweet soul? You bet.

—WASHINGTON, DC, 1950

IN MEMORY OF TERESA ŻARNOWER

Without friends or relatives in the great, great city,
Which is a gigantic cemetery of mad ships,
Teresa was dying. She had no strength
To conquer the past with her already cooling hands.
They found her when they opened the door in the morning
Lying in a great silence and a disorder of appliances.
And someone covered her eyes with a handkerchief.

In that far-off great city, where everyone treads
Carefully and craftily because they know what it means
To merge with the silent wave of private despair.
With black dust, oblivion, the filth of poor neighborhoods,
Where so many faiths have been annulled, so many secrets,
In that far-off great city where the livid light
Of stone tunnels strikes fear by night,
And naked manikins cast shadows with their pointy breasts,
Where dawn arrives first at the height of a hundred floors,
Teresa had been dying—for years, not hours.

Every piece of news that came to her across the ocean
About the exiled, the poisoned, the burned alive,
Was like a last sign—and the world took its leave of her
And there was no flight from the losses
Until, like a pine in the debris under a downpour,
She stood under the city lights, a sad, black tree.

Her good hands have been taken from us.
The waters have closed over her life and work.
Cast a handful of flowers, passerby, on an extinguished name.

—WASHINGTON, DC, 1950

MARSH (ZUŁAWY)

Sleep, gold, in the rich, black earth. Metal
With the worn-thin head of a prince, a lion, a crown, sleep.
Someone there was assigned to unearth you
And you will ornament museums in my country.

Heavy clocks, silver tureens, trunks of hammered metal
Flow now among forgotten stars,
Flash and vanish in the abyss of time.
Let what must pass pass quickly.

Here a truck rumbles along an empty highway.
The earth arises slowly from the marshes.
Seagulls carry white wings over gray waters.
The wind kindles a low red sun in the grass.

Here the rust of wrecked machines, lashed by rain
Under the black sails of the windmills beyond the dike,
And, boarding the ferry, a small shaggy horse,
With shaft-bow and shafts, skids on the wet planks.

People who never knew wealth or power
Sat down to a lamp and old, cracked walls.
Their faces are ashen from the bad years.
The road they traveled already obliterated.

What to wish such a person? May he be happy.
May he create marvels with his own hands.
And plough up not gold but the stuff of dreams.

May he change these wetlands retrieved from water and flame
Into a dark green garden by thought alone.
Thunder. At the mouth of the Vistula the foaming sea.

—WASHINGTON, DC, 1950

THREE CHORUSES FROM AN UNWRITTEN DRAMA "HIROSHIMA"

1

What I speak of happened.
When the fruit of the apple tree gave no sweetness to the lips,
When the heart beat irregularly, when men
Knew that something was very wrong,

They traveled earth's roads without the strength to sing.
The great war had ended and still it continued on the islands.
Fish knocked against the windows of drowned ships.

Words or pictures? You can see how the hangars
In that airport glisten. There are groves of palms
Beyond which the sea crashes in milky foam
Also wide asphalt roads and beyond them
The heavy machines descending through pure azure.

As always the plant life, there where the bulldozers
Crushed the hot, primeval forest, is attempting to regain
Its lost nests, entwines itself around rusted tin cans,
Creeps over gasoline cans, and with its tiny leaves
Rattles against the canvas of the soldiers' tents.

The soldiers, who are spending their youth here,
Dream dreams of rainbow-colored girls
In the drone of mosquitoes, in the intermissions
Between meting out this death and the next.
A full moon wanes above the cries of the nightbirds.

2

So what is it that I want to say here? I have come
To the middle of my life. The force of it
Seethes in me, carries me, gathers my thoughts
And I search in vain for words to bear witness.
The gleam in a pair of human eyes is more beautiful
To me than all the stars in the heavens. The granularity
Of a hand, the fragile shape of a neck, the lathe
Of a knee are more amazing to me than a tree in blossom.

So many times I've walked in the crowds in great cities,
Called there by the warm power of my blood, by desire,
Wishing to gather and to seal in myself forever
The fates of all the people, hungering to be at the same time
Man and woman, a child and an old one, to strengthen
The voices of my brothers and sisters with my call,
To embrace every silence, every smile. And to enter
This way the fiery center where human beings live.

So what is it that I want to say? The work is done.
A shadow has moved across the sundial,
The century and the year and the month and the hour.
The plane descended, shrill in the serene blue of the sky.
Its engines thundered, fell silent, the wheels jerked
earthward, the blades of the propellors
Made broken rainbows as the plane touched ground,
Jumped, touched ground again, the motors roaring
As it turned in the grassy verge of the field, shuddered
And grew still, and the young fliers, disembarking,
Went to their headquarters to file a longer report than usual.

3

Who is thinking of the dead? Light green pastures
Steam in the sloping fields of Michigan. In the morning fog
You hear the cry of wild geese, flying north
Over the Great Lakes to the marshes of Labrador,
Once long ago deer passed by on this trail,
Drowsy flotillas of wandering buffalo,
There were beaver towns, grayish thickets
In which wild turkey kept their leks. Today
The geese fly over the rivery patterns of railroad tracks,
Over the lines on highways where the lights
Of early traffic and the sanguinary eyes of taillights
Taxi through morning mist. They pass by aluminum,
Concrete, steel, fly over the shining surfaces
Of water. They place sentries and guard a law
That has lasted for thousands and thousands of years.
Now is the hour when, from the locomotive
The hand of the engineer emerges holding a cup of coffee,
When in the violet chapels of Amoco and Esso
The watchmen of the gasoline rite doze off
With their heads on their elbows under the shields of clocks.
Now is the hour when at the edge of cities,
In the aridity of scrap iron and cardboard,
Dark figures kindle campfires
And on cables above the luster of avenues
The spark of acetylene crackles and dies.
Day, day. A red-breasted thrush
Standing straight on a maple branch
Rises from song. Transparent song.
Brilliant song. And the steady drip of dew,
Trickling, chasing itself. Oh light, oh day.
Sun, day. A day of spring.

—PARIS, 1950

"It's always bad in Eastern Europe.
In Eastern Europe *things happen.*
It's always unpleasant in Eastern Europe.
One minute there is a person, and the next minute there isn't.
And so, dear daughter, avoid it as much as you can,
And don't tell anyone you come from Eastern Europe."

So Mrs. Baker murmurs to her daughter Katrine
As she pours coffee from a shiny machine.
Her husband's name is Piekorz.
Although he dug black coal from the earth,
He was a quiet man with a peasant's heart,
Born somewhere near Mielec.
Mrs. Baker's father went to Saxony for summer work.
He plowed the fields of Brandenburg.
Mrs. Baker's mother herded sheep in her bare feet.
In the drowsy old country, in a small village in the Tatras.
The shepherd's song warmed her on chilly mornings,
A song that moved Mrs. Baker not in the least.

With her elbows on the counter, slowly drinking coffee,
She looks through the window at an autumnal scene:
Green roofs with a neon logo,
An Amoco station and next to it an Esso,
And where October has altered the maple trees,
A dark red forest spills down the mountainside,
Touched by a faint bluish haze,
As if it were a scene from a magic lantern.
Below the forest a massive gray slag heap
Like the wall of an abandoned fortress,
And cranes circling in incessant motion
And a drift of smoke the wind is scattering.

Lower on the slope, tiny houses run—
White trifles, as if cut out with a jigsaw,
And in the distance among the trees
Shines a little mining town on a river.

—WASHINGTON, DC, 1950

YOU WHO WRONGED

You who wronged a simple man
Bursting into laughter at the crime,
And kept a pack of fools around you
To mix good and evil, to blur the line,

Though everyone bowed down before you,
Saying virtue and wisdom lit your way,
Striking gold medals in your honor,
Glad to have survived another day,

Do not feel safe. The poet remembers.
You can kill one, but another is born.
The words are written down, the deed, the date.

And you'd have done better with a winter dawn,
A rope, and a branch bowed beneath your weight.

—WASHINGTON, DC, 1950

1951, EUROPE

ENTOMBED IN THEIR ANCESTORS

des nobles insensés
Enseverlis dan leurs ancêtres
　—ANDRÉ CHÉNIER

They gambled their home away. Snow blew away the borders.
The troops arrived from Petersburg with a fife
And the Asiatic horse entered their capital.
The blood of the angry mob grew cold on the pikes.

They rose up in battle, they lost the Uprising,
Because they were afraid to arm their peasants.
The wind drove them into the snow, carried them over the ocean
They dreamed at night of the brilliance of the hangman's noose.

The Tsar freed the peasant to their despite.
Money built forges and workshops.
The half-naked seasonal workers escaped to the factories
And fled from their miserable huts to foreign lands.

Once again they had a state, but it did not last long.
The Uhlan horses pranced in review.
They changed what could have been glory into vainglory.
Both shade and death lay down in their history.

The Muscovite drove into the ruins of the city in tanks.
He gave them laws and put collars on them.
A new province is already growing in the Imperium,
Bearing coal, tallow, and grain in tribute.

The folk curse their lot and clowns sing to them
That they have never been so free as today.
So they search the sky to read the future.
The peace of servility? Or annihilation in war?

And the nobles, meanwhile, shivering in their caves of darkness,
Pass judgment, not knowing that they are already judged.

—PARIS, 1951

PARIS, 1951

With what song, City, to sing
The violet of Byzantine twilights,
The shadow of the sword that cuts
In two necklaces of dark gold.
How to bring a gift of song
Different from the days of ancient glory,
To put away in a locked chest
The eagles and torn standards?

I drive in anger from Garenne-Bezons,
A thousand bicycles hurry past,
Wind under the bridges blows smoke
From the barges, billows the linens.
In the hour of violet fog
Thousands and thousands of them hurry past,
Shoulders bent, bag on the diagonal
Over the handlebars of the bicycles,
The faces and hands of my brothers,
The gaze of my brothers.

City of my regrets,
Cruel, sweet, and human,
Rose that burns the heart
For the price of meat and wine,
For the price of humiliation,
For the price of tears and hope.

Time was showering leaves
Over L'Île Saint-Louis,
Erased kisses in the dark
At the hour of violet fog
Over the water
Under the glow of the lights.
Our bedsheets carted in baskets
To and from laundries where
Traces of her lipstick were washed away
And the shape of her sleeping head.

Trumpets had played, and flutes.
They fell silent. Years went by.
I returned, not the same person,
To your sour streets.

To sing, City, another song
Of its epoch and the dust it sheds
So that there remains in the museums
A breath of bleached silk,
An armchair with arms no longer warm,
The rustle of bygone gowns,
and a little bowl of dried mascara
under the dark theater of a mirror.

It's not true. That's not what remains.
Wind thrashes the surface of the river,
A thousand bicycles hurry past,
The wind toward Porte Clignancourt.
What begins in our hands,
And from our hearts,
Will last longer than an echo,
Longer than a falling star.

O my friends,
Speakers of different languages,
If we are given disaster,
A dream will outlast it,
A scream that will, at least once,
Penetrate millions of those
Who live on earth.

To sing me a new song
In the hour when those who keep silent
In the lands east and west
And on the shores of a bloody sea,
Try to hide from others with their hands
The source that beats in their chests,
The hot and nameless
Source of a guarded hope.

—PARIS, 1951

MITTELBERGHEIM

Wine sleeps in casks of Rhine oak.
I am wakened by the bell of a chapel in the vineyards
Of Mittelbergheim. I hear a small spring
Trickling into a well in the yard, a clatter
Of sabots in the street. Tobacco drying
Under the eaves, and ploughs and wooden wheels
And mountain slopes and autumn are with me.

I keep my eyes closed. Do not rush me,
You, fire, power, might, for it is too early.
I have lived through many years and, as in this half dream,
I felt I was attaining the moving frontier
Beyond which color and sound come true
And the things of this earth are united.
Do not yet force me to open my lips.
Let me trust and believe I will attain.
Let me linger here in Mittelbergheim.

I know I should. They are with me,
Autumn and wooden wheels and tobacco hung
Under the eaves. Here and everywhere
Is my homeland, wherever I turn
And in whatever language I would hear
The song of a child, the conversation of lovers.
Happier than anyone, I am to receive
A glance, a smile, a star, silk creased
At the knee. Serene, beholding,
I am to walk on hills in the soft glow of day
Over waters, cities, roads, human customs.

Fire, power, might, you who hold me
In the palm of your hand whose furrows
Are like immense gorges combed
By southern wind. You who grant certainty
In the hour of fear, in the week of doubt,
It is too early, let the wine mature,
Let the travelers sleep in Mittelbergheim.

    —ALSACE, 1951

1952–1953: EUROPE

THE FAUST OF WARSAW

By the murmur of the fountain in Luxembourg Garden,
Where a sailboat floats on the waters,
Pushed by a child's hand, I think of you.

In the blue light, in the constellation of the leaves
You, standing before me, Faust, for whom
The elixir of youth did not suffice.
You who demanded order and power.
I draw a line in the sand and you appear
And I ask you, what right do you have
To lie to yourself and to give your fear
The name of order and power?

Fear: that one might fall among those who live
As water lives in overgrown gardens,
In the darkness of ruins, whose blind endurance
Is the fulfillment of death before they die.

I know that you don't think much of human strength.
You demean yourself by believing that no one now
Is going to escape the fate of those exiles
Who have rejected the greatest gift: their own minds.

Fear: that their hands will reach us, the traffickers
In reputation, the executioners,
Murderers *pro procuram*. But that's how it is.
Those who write anything in the Polish tongue
other than tender odes, threatening to no one,
Can expect nothing in return but hatred.

Fear: that the judgment will fall—of History,
You say, shrugging your shoulders. Look,
Here, in this garden I held her hand,
Her body was like the body of a swallow
Fluttering inside my palm. And she's dead.
I don't even know whether you can say
That Charon's boat carried her into the darkness,
Because there was barbed wire, feces, blood,
Before the miraculous mechanism of burning
Sparks, thoughts, desires, inspirations
Falls apart and is returned to earth.
Tell me why I should not, in the moment
Given to me, pay back the debt owed to those
Who did not get to experience the ripeness
Of living out a life? And then let the terror
Called History overtake them.

Fear: the chauffeur hits the horn, and on the run
You see the grayed ruins of Wola,
The scaffolds, the dust and bricks. The poor crowd,
   the gray crowd
Wobbles from leg to leg, standing in lines.
You wipe your forehead with a foreign handkerchief.
Sorcerer, you know the penalty that comes down,
The penalty born in the smoke of this century,
That explodes like a flash of magnesium, and persists,
O let it be accursed—consciousness.

    —PARIS, 1952

NOTEBOOK: EUROPE

It's undermined—the Gotthard Tunnel.
Where wool sleeps
And children's breath stirs the wings of paper butterflies,
Where on the edges of fountains wet horses
Rear in the May air,
Where they were able to lay cable underground.

It's undermined—our native realm,
Not large, sweet for us, European.
Olives are grown there, and grain,
The wind runs through fields of flax
And quiets in the black leaves of an orange grove.

It's undermined—the blue sea,
In the hour when the cutter goes out for fishing
From the little town where cats sleep among the nets.

Man's heart is undermined.
The time given him for life, and another time
Are in his consciousness like two lines
Instead of being one, in harmony.

—PARIS, 1952

NOTEBOOK: DORDOGNE

Bird, deer, fawn-colored beasts
Think they do not return to their ancestors.
Bird, deer, fawn-colored beasts
Live and die, and they don't know time.

On the Weser, under the rocks
People walk through the vineyards,
Carry baskets full of apples
Gathered from the great apple trees.

On the Weser castles shine,
And higher, sculpted into the rock,
A sentinel lookout stands,
From the last war, a hundred years ago.

On the Gallo-Roman arches
Itinerant leaves of ivy.
Women wash linens
In the sunny waters of the Weser.

Whether with sadness or with joy,
They have found a stone arrowhead
And given the stone arrowhead
To the girl at the museum gate.

—LES EYZIES, 1952

NOTEBOOK: BONS BY LAKE LEMAN

Red beeches, shining poplars
And steep spruce behind October fog.
In the valley the lake steams. There is snow
Already on the hillsides of the other shore.
Of life, what remains? Only this light
So that the eyes blink in the sunny noon
Of such a season. People say: this is,
And no capacity, no artfulness
Can reach beyond what is.
And memory, useless, loses its power.

Kegs smell of cider. The vicar mixes lime
With a spade in front of the school.
My son runs there on the path. Boys carry
Sacks of chestnuts gathered on the slope.
If I forget thee, Jerusalem,
Says the prophet, let my right hand wither.
Underground tremors shake what is.
Mountains crack and forests break.
Touched by what was and what will be,
All that is crumbles into dust.
Violent, clean, the world is again in ferment
And neither ambition nor memory ceases.

Autumnal skies, the same in childhood,
In adulthood and old age. I won't
Stare at you. And you, landscapes,
Nourishing our hearts with mild warmth,
What poison dwells in you that you seal our lips,
Makes us sit with folded arms and the look
Of sleepy animals? Whoever finds order,
Peace, and an eternal moment in what is
Will vanish without a trace. Do you agree then
To abolish what is, and pluck from movement
The eternal moment as a gleam
On the current of the black river? I do.

    —BONS, 1953

NOTES

CM visited Rome in 1937, and this poem suggests that his mind was still in Europe in 1946. The mysterious imagery seems to be very much in the manner of the symbolic and semi-allegorical poems he wrote in the 1930s.

At the globe's still point, where the Tiber unravels time: CM translated T. S. Eliot's "Burnt Norton," which contains these lines:

> *At the still point of the turning world. Neither flesh nor fleshless:*
> *Neither from nor toward; at the still point, there the dance is.*

The Polish phrase that he used to render "still point," *nieruchomego punktu*, is the same one that he uses here. The passage in "Burnt Norton" continues:

> *Except for the point, the still point,*
> *There would be no dance, and there is only the dance.*

On the Song of a Bird on the Banks of the Potomac

This poem is written in a formal meter, a four-stress, eleven-syllable line.

Recall Ponary, yellow with young leaves: The Ponary hills had many associations for the residents of Wilno (Vilnius). To the young CM they were a place for hiking.

On the road from Jazuny, as Slowacki once did?: Juliuz Slowacki was a major Polish poet of the Romantic period and a resident of Wilno. The Philomaths were a secret society at the University of Wilno, created in 1817 by, among others, Adam Mickiewicz with the aim of freeing Lithuania and Poland from the Russian Empire.

A Reminder

Six stanzas of six syllable lines. Irregularly rhymed. The context is the Greek Civil War. Tony Judt, *Postwar: A History of Europe Since 1945*: "Greece—like Yugoslavia—experienced World War Two as a cycle of invasion, occupation, resistance, reprisals, and civil war, culminating in five weeks of clashes in Athens between Communists and the royalist-backed British forces in December 1944, after which an armistice was agreed upon in February 1945. Fighting broke out again, however, in 1946 and lasted for three more years, ending with a rout of the Communists from their strongholds in the mountainous north. . . . The KKE (Communist) guerillas and the Athens-based and western-backed government of the king terrorized villages, destroyed communications, and divided the country for decades to come. By the time the war was over, in September 1949, 10 percent of the population was homeless" (35).

Treatise on Morals

"*Traktat Moralny*" was written in 1957 in Washington, DC, where CM was serving as cultural attaché at the embassy of the People's Republic of Poland. This long poem was written in a regular eleven-syllable line, with rhymed couplets, and what has been described as the raucous rhythm of a Krakow cabaret song. It addresses the question of whether any system of morality has survived the war and how to listen to stories about the war and the ideological positions that were starting to contend with one another in explaining it. The poem was published in a journal in Poland—it was clearly a tour de force—and led to his recall by his employers and his ultimate defection from the People's Republic.

A note on the notes: most of the general cultural references in the poem—to Herodotus, Sartre, we have assumed to be available to readers of this poem and we've not annotated the poem in that way. We did, however, translate a couple of Latin phrases.

Just what, o poet, do you propose to save? The Polish line is simpler: "Where, poet, is rescue?" The translators' expansion was an effort to capture the sense of challenge with which the poem begins. The Polish word for "save" or "rescue" is "*ocalenie*," and it is the title of the book of poems from the war years that CM published in 1945. This quoted voice with which the poem begins may be an allusion to Dominik Horodynski's review of the book *Where is Rescue?*

They cite him expressis verbis: Latin, "in one's express words."

And they put a volume of the encyclopedia / In the pot: In a Polish interview, CM remarks that he had *Gulliver's Travels* in mind and Laputa, a land where "everything is calculated precisely but there is nothing to eat."

Die *gigantic* Liquidation: The German phrase means "closing-out sale."

With a quill, a revolver, or a shovel: The Polish word "*naganem*" would have called to mind a German service pistol.

You live here, now. Hic et nunc: Latin, "here and now."

Don't say: the convention of the long knives: An allusion to the "night of the long knives," June 30, 1934, during which, on Hitler's orders, some 150 members of the internal opposition were murdered by the SS.

The posthumous hiccup of Heidelberg: The two major philosophical movements to emerge in Europe after the war were French existentialism and German phenomenology. Karl Jaspers, one of the founding figures in phenomenology, along with Edmund Husserl and Martin Heidegger, was a professor at the University of Heidelberg from 1922 to 1937, when he was forced to resign his position because his wife was Jewish.

In spite of all, the Ding an Sich: German, "the thing in itself," a term used by Immanuel Kant in his *Critique of Pure Reason* (1781).

They found this: Être pour Soi: French, "existence for oneself." A concept from Jean-Paul Sartre's *Being and Nothingness* (1943).

And the Sartrean contradiction is alien to him: The conflict between Sartre's notions of *être pour soir* (being for oneself) and *être en soir* (being in oneself) was a topic, as was Sartre's philosophy of freedom and his Stalinism.

And Bergson again, élan vital: Henri Bergson was a prominent French philosopher of the 1910s and 1920s. *Élan vital,* "vital force," was his term for the life force in all living things. This passage is a riff on fashionable contemporary French and German thought, about which Polish writers found reason, in the aftermath of the war, to be skeptical.

A misadventure occurred in Cracow: Krakow, relatively undamaged by the war, became a center of resistance to Soviet rule in Poland. In 1947 it was associated with Roman Catholic conservatism.

Here at home, Witkiewicz is an interesting case: Stanisław Witkiewicz (1859–1939) was a writer, painter, and creator of avant-garde theater. He committed suicide in September 1939 upon hearing that the Red Army was crossing the border into Poland.

Than that the tropical moss of unwashed souls: A paraphrase of the title of an ironic treatise by Stanisław Witkiewicz, titled "Unwashed Souls," written in 1936.

If I believe in finis terrae: Latin, "the end of the earth," i.e., of the world.

In two, into flower and root: Most probably an allusion to a formulation of Stanisław Brzozowski (1878–1911): "Romanticism is the rebellion of the flower against the roots," from his book *The Legend of Young Poland* (1911).

Where demons on infernal couches: In *Conversations with Czesław Miłosz*, eds. Ewa Czaenecka and Aleksander Fiut, CM comments of these lines: "Here, for example, I am writing about the security police." The Urząd Bezpieczeństwa was the Polish KGB.

Is séparé de lui-même: French, "separated from himself."

Avoid those who in their own circle, playing the political horses: Also from *Conversations with Czesław Miłosz:* "This fragment is about Gomulka." Władysław Gomułka (1905–1982) was First Secretary of the Polish United Workers Party, 1956–70. In 1947–48, he was the de facto leader of postwar Poland.

Thus with a Sarmatian relish: The Sarmatians were a nomadic, horse-riding people of Iranian origin who came into southeastern Europe in the fourth century AD. The Polish nobility liked to claim a Sarmatian origin.

La civilization des punaises: French, "civilization of bedbugs," evidently a French traveler's slander.

And the rescue is in you alone: The word "*ocalenie,*" with which the poem begins by asking, "Where is rescue?"

Summer Movies in Central Park

A formal poem, rhymed quatrains, eleven-syllable lines.

For Juliusz Kronski in Paris: Julusz Kronski, CM's friend and antagonist, known as Tiger, was a Marxist intellectual with whom Miłosz struggled over the issue of historical determinism.

Here, in the line of cars along 5th Avenue: Arriving in New York in 1946, CM was first assigned to the Polish consulate in Manhattan. He and his wife were given an apartment on the Upper West Side. He walked across the park mornings and evenings to work in the offices at Lexington Avenue on the East Side.

Untitled

CM visited San Francisco in June 1948 in the company of Wanda Telakowska, a painter and sculptor. Their mission for the Ministry of Culture was to promote high-quality Polish fabric designs. As this poem suggests, they visited Fisherman's Wharf. He could not have known that he would be living in the region for forty years.

The People's Graphic Workshop (*El Taller de Gráfica Popular*)

This poem was written in 1948. The People's Graphic Workshop was an artists' collective founded by several Mexican painters in 1937 for the purpose of making a revolutionary popular art through the medium of inexpensive printing. They had some association with David Siqueiros and the Mexican muralist movement and with the group who plotted the assassination of Leon Trotsky in 1940. CM never visited Mexico.

A Concert

This poem is metrical and intricately rhymed. CM remarked to RG that the poem records an experience of attending a concert and having a sudden vision of the musicians as busy insects. He didn't say whether he had also then the vision of the fashionably dressed dead looking up at the spectacle.

To Tadeusz Różewicz, Poet

Tadeusz Różewicz (1921–2014) belongs to the remarkable generation of Polish poets, including Zbigniew Herbert and Wisława Szymborska, born during the time of Polish independence and coming of age during the war. Różewicz published his first book of poems, *Anxiety*, in 1947, the year before this poem was written.

The poem, like Różewicz's, is unrhymed, but the tone of it is in striking contrast to the younger poet's. Here are a few lines from "Survivor," a poem in *Anxiety:*

> *I'm searching for a teacher and a master.*
> *let him give me back my sight hearing and speech*
> *let him name objects and concepts again*
> *let him separate the light from the dark*
>
> *I'm twenty-four*
> *Led to slaughter*
> *I survived*

To Albert Einstein

Miłosz met Einstein several times in the course of his diplomatic work. In the summer of 1950, he asked Einstein's advice and explained his torment in his current role. Einstein advised him not to sever ties with his language.

My Mother's Grave

A poem in seven numbered parts (an ode form), sixteen to twenty lines in each section, classic eleven-syllable line. CM's mother died in 1945 in a village in the marshlands of the Baltic coast.

To Laura

A formal poem in quatrains, rhymed abab. Irregular line length. In the style of the eighteenth-century poet Franciszek Karpiński. His most popular poem involves a "Laura." The first line of the poem comes from Karpinski. It seems CM is playing with the sentimental ballad to make a political poem. "Laura" is probably CM's wife, Janka.

Siegfried and Erika

I'm aware of three poems by Tadeusz Borowski, written from a DP camp, that use the image of German girls consorting with Black GIs as symbols of the humiliation of the German people. Here the speaker is German. The author doesn't necessarily own the attitude. There is on the internet a thesis by Jamie Christopher Morris, *The Black Experience in Postwar Germany* (https//opencommons .uconn.edu/srhonors_theses/224).

This poem was written in Washington in 1949, Miłosz in the postwar taking on the subject of the German experience of the war. Prosodically I'm not sure about it, unrhymed, a mix of nine- and eleven-syllable lines, I think, perhaps in imitation of the German elegy. In the poem, Siegfried is speaking.

A Thought About Asia

That sound from the depth of antediluvian rocks: strongly resembles the sound heard in the Marabar Caves in E. M. Forster's *A Passage to India* (1924). The dismantling of colonial empires was another dynamic of the period.

A Little Negro Girl Playing Chopin

CM, like other European visitors to the United States after WWII (Federico García Lorca, Albert Camus) was fascinated by what he saw of African American culture and had some of the typical European prejudices. "Only the Negroes," he wrote, after a quick look around New York City, "have souls." Part of his work as a cultural attaché was to report on American culture and in a book of his translations published in 1953, he printed some translations of African American poets and more than a dozen examples of the African American spiritual, struck by the way that the language of Jewish slavery in Egypt gave the enslaved Africans a coded language in which to talk about their condition.

In the nineteenth century, Poland had been carved up for a hundred years by the Habsburg, Prussian, and Russian Tsarist empires, and by the end of the century all of Chopin's music was associated with the Polish dream of liberation, so a Black girl in the United States playing the music of a dream of freedom had at least a double meaning for Polish readers. Or triple: serfdom was abolished in Polish and Lithuanian territories under foreign control in the middle of the nineteenth century, so a complicated history is gathered in this portrait of a young Black girl in Washington, DC, playing a European étude.

We were of two minds about how to present this poem. The description of the young pianist's racial markers—shiny teeth, nappy hair—which would have been fascinating physical facts to Northern Europeans with not much experience of people from tropical Africa, feels racist in the United States in the twenty-first century. It is certainly racial, and it's certain that the author intended no derogation. On the contrary. And so translators may well have felt justified in presenting this English version of the Polish poem:

> *If only you had seen her, Sir Frederick,*
> *How she placed her fingers on the keys*
> *And diligently bent her head to the keyboard,*
>
> *How she placed her slender foot on the pedal,*
>
> *Comically childlike, in a well-trodden little shoe,*
>
> *And when the hall suddenly went quiet,*
> *The primrose of tone slowly unfurled.*
>
> *If only you had seen in the hall, in the semidarkness,*

The firmness of her lips, the small smile
When the grand piano bore your cares
And how the music fell in slanting ribbons,

And how through stained glass and a chorus of bird song,

It was spring in a city unknown to you by name,
If only you had seen how those tones flew,
Pulled motes of dust and a shaft of sunlight

Across her solemn face, as it rested in her palms,

Surely you would have said it was worth it.

For CM and the Negro spiritual, see Katarzyna Jakubiak, "Translation's Deceit: Czesław Miłosz and Negro Spirituals," *Przekładaniec* 25 (2013): 199–220.

He Has No Sight

The English word "girl" occurs twice in the poem to describe the elevator operator, but not in the seventh stanza. CM was reading Henry Miller's 1941 book *The Air-Conditioned Nightmare*, which may have had some influence in this poem.

This description from *Native Realm* of the origin of the poem provides some insight into the complexity of his situation: He is discussing his relationship with his friend, a Marxist philosopher: "Tiger forbade me to publish certain poems. For example, the poem I wrote after a stopover in Detroit. After being taken up to the twentieth floor by the hotel porter, I sat in my plush, overheated room, near the radio trickling music, and looked down at the neons below me, the garages, the traffic—metal fish circulating in an aquarium—and was so powerfully struck by the universal blunting of human desires here that an image crossed my mind of a man being sucked out from the inside as one sucks out an egg through a straw. And from that image came a poem about a man torn from himself, about alienation. No political motives prompted me. Tiger, however, was of the opinion that the specialists in anti-Americanism would be too pleased by the work and would pervert my intention by reading into it a zealot bend to Party directives."

Carolers

This songlike poem belongs to Christmas lore and pre-Christian rituals surrounding the winter solstice. Kolednicy, the title of the Polish poem, are carolers, groups of people who go from house to house in costume between Christmas and Epiphany, singing in exchange for sweets, or, as the poem has it, a tithe of seasonal foods.

With bagpipes, fifes, and the horns of a bull: The "bull," a turon in Polish, is a mythical beast with the head of an auroch, a long-extinct European bison (such as were drawn on the walls of caves in Europe since the Ice Age).

Miłosz, it would seem, is in Washington, DC, turning out a celebratory poem without irony. He himself belonged to Polish Lithuania rather than the holiday rituals of rural central Poland.

The six stanzas of the poem have an abab rhyme scheme and a refrain.

To Myself, for an Album, New Year's 1950

This poem is written in rhymed quatrains, and very fluent thirteen-syllable lines.

In Memory of Teresa Żarnower

Teresa Żarnower (1897–1949) was an artist, sculptor, designer, and a major figure in the Polish avant-garde in the first half of the twentieth century. She came from an assimilated Jewish family and left Poland in 1937 for Paris, Spain, and eventually New York, where she died, apparently by suicide, in her apartment at 15 West 57th Street.

You will be blessed by both Piast and Rzepicha: Piast is the mythic founder of the Polish state. Rzepicha was his wife.

Marsh (Żuławy)

Seven stanzas of thirteen-syllable lines, intricately rhymed. Żuławy might also be translated as "fen" or "fenlands." The scene is the Baltic coast, near to where Miłosz's mother died and was buried.

Three Choruses from an Unwritten Drama "Hiroshima"

The *Enola Gay* took off from an airfield in the Mariana Islands in August 1945.

Entombed in Their Ancestors

The poem is a capsule history of the Polish aristocracy and takes its title from the lines by the eighteenth-century French poet André Chénier: "these foolish nobles buried in their ancestors." Like Chénier's critique of the French nobility, this is an account of the large landowning class who dominated Polish politics for several centuries. "The troops" in the second line are the arrival of the Russian empire in the eighteenth century. Tsar Nicholas freed the Polish serfs in 1863. The former serfs became workers in the new factories. The poem can't have won CM friends in the Polish émigré communities in Europe and the US. The poem was written in Paris in 1951. That is, having rejected the Polish Communist government, he published this sardonic rejection of the Polish right.

Paris, 1951

CM first lived in Paris for a year, as a scholarship student in 1934–35, and returned to Paris in 1951, when he defected.

I drive in anger from Garenne-Bezons: A northeastern suburb of Paris.
To sing me a new song: Echoes in Psalms 96 and 98.

The Faust of Warsaw

You see the grayed ruins of Wola: The Wola Massacre was the systematic murder of between forty thousand and fifty thousand Polish people in the Wola neighborhood of Warsaw by the German Wehrmacht and fellow Axis collaborators in the Azerbaijani Legion, as well as the mostly Russian RONA forces. It took place between the fifth to twelfth of August 1944. The massacre was ordered by Adolf Hitler, who directed his armies to kill "anything that moves" in order to stop the Warsaw Uprising as soon as it began.

Notebook: Bons by Lake Leman

Miłosz first lived in Paris for a year, as a scholarship student in 1934–35, and returned to Paris in 1951, where he defected.

Miłosz and his family had been separated for thirty-three months, during which he had acted out the drama of his break with the Polish government and with the European intellectuals who supported Joseph Stalin's Soviet Union. Reunited with his wife, Janka, and his son, Anthony, he came directly to the small village of Bons on the French side of Lake Geneva.

*P*OET IN THE NEW WORLD was the idea of David
Frick, a scholar of Polish literature and culture who had re-
placed Czesław Miłosz in the UC Berkeley Department of
Slavic Languages and Literatures and had recently retired. Like
me, he was very interested in the poems Czesław wrote between
1946, when he left Poland and came to the United States as a young
diplomat, and 1953, when, having left the United States, he re-
turned to Europe, resigned from his position, and defected from
the People's Republic. Unlike me, David could read the poems,
and he proposed that we collaborate on English translations.

I was particularly interested in the long poem "*Traktat Moralny*,"
or "Treatise on Morals," because several of the books about his
poems written in Polish and translated into English referred to
the poem. I had worked with Czesław on the translation of his
"Treatise on Poetry," written in the later 1950s, and his "Treatise on
Theology," written near the end of his life, and making a version
of this other treatise felt like it was completing a part of the record.
Czesław and I had, in fact, taken a look at the idea of translating
"Treatise on Morals" and given up almost immediately. The poem
was written in rhymed couplets. He felt that the translation had to
rhyme if it was going to convey what the author was up to, and he
hated translations of his work that didn't say in English more or
less exactly what the Polish said. So we gave up. David thought that

a translation that aimed to say more or less exactly what the Polish said, was possible, and would at least convey to new readers Miłosz's state of mind in the aftermath of a war that destroyed cities and killed millions of people. So we set out to render the poem and, while we were at it, translate most of the poems Czesław wrote in those years.

David had done first rough translations of all the poems and we had worked together at making satisfactory and fairly literal versions of about a third of them, when he died suddenly, peacefully, in his sleep. Czesław's longtime editor Daniel Halpern encouraged me to finish the project. For that purpose I was very fortunate to have the help of two native speakers of Polish and immensely subtle readers of Czesław's poems, Renata Gorczyńska and Karol Berger. I could not have proceeded without them. I am also grateful to Peter Dale Scott, who was in the process of finishing his brilliant study of Miłosz, *Ecstatic Pessimist*, and Murray Silverstein, David Shaddock, and Jesse Nathan, who joined Peter and me to read through some of the poems. Paul Ebenkamp supplied a poet's eye and editorial order to assembling the final manuscript and giving another look at what we had done with the poems in English.

David Frick was a scholar and meticulous. His field was religion and community in Poland and Lithuania in the seventeenth century, and his book reconstructing almost street by street the religious and practical life of the city of Vilnius and its many communities of belief has been described as "a masterpiece of urban geography." David's idea of translation involved, he had told me, bringing the reader to the poem. My inclination was to bring the poem to the reader. All of the poems Czesław wrote in those years were, to my surprise, written in formal measures. Most of them are rhymed. So we worked our way through the poems at the dining room table of David's bayside home while his very charming and completely undisciplined Jack Russell terrier tried to distract us. We tried to be as literal as possible, tried to represent something of the feel of the movement of the poems and their syntax. David had intended to follow *Poet in the New World* with a book about the times, the evaluation of his diplomatic work by embassy officials, his letters home, and the political and personal milieu in which he was working at what was a dramatic moment in the history of the twentieth century. We have lost that book. But he has given us this one.

FURTHER READINGS

Czesław Miłosz, *The Captive Mind* (1953)

Czesław Miłosz, *The Seizure of Power* (1955)

Czesław Miłosz, *Native Realm* (1959)

Andrzej Franaszek, *Miłosz: A Biography*
(Cambridge, MA: Harvard University Press, 2017)

Ewa Kołodziejczyk, *Czesław Miłosz in Postwar America*
(Berlin: De Gruyter, 2021)

Peter Dale Scott, *Ecstatic Pessimist: Czeslaw Milosz,
Poet of Catastrophe and Hope* (Lanham, MD: Rowman
& Litlefield, 2022)

Tony Judt, *Postwar: A History of Europe Since 1945*
(New York: Penguin, 2005)

Norman Davies, *God's Playground: A History of Poland, Vol. II*
(New York: Columbia University Press, 2005)

INDEX OF TRANSLATORS

DF: DAVID FRICK

RH: ROBERT HASS

RP: ROBERT PINSKY

JD: JAN DAROWSKY

PDS: PETER DALE SCOTT

JC: JOHN CARPENTER

RL: RICHARD LOURIE

RB: RICHARD BERENGARTEN

GG: GEORGE GOMORI

Editor's note: The poems not previously translated are those by DF and RH. "To Jonathan Swift" was translated by CM and RH but not previously published. "Antigone," translated by GG and RB, was published in the *Hungarian Quarterly* in Budapest in 2001.

"Earth": CM/RH

"A Family": CM/RH

"The Faust of Warsaw": DF/RH

"He Has No Sight": DF/RH

"In Memory of Teresa Żarnower": DF/RH

"The Journey": CM/RH

"A Legend": CM/RH

"A Little Negro Girl Playing Chopin": DF/RH

"Marsh": DF/RH

"Mittelbergheim": CM/RL

"My Mother's Grave": DF/RH

"Notebook: Bons by Lake Leman": DF/RH

"Notebook: Dordogne": DF/RH

"Notebook: Europe": DF/RH

"Notebook: Pennsylvania": DF/RH

"Ocean": PDS

"On the Song of a Bird on the Banks of the Potomac": DF/RH

"The Palace of My Muses": DF/RH

"Paris, 1951": DF/RH

"Reflections": DF/RH

"A Reminder": DF/RH

"Siegfried and Erika": DF/RH

"Song on Porcelain": CM/RP

"The Spirit of the Laws": JC

"Summer Movies in Central Park": DF/RH

"A Thought About Asia": DF/RH

"Three Choruses from an Unwritten Drama 'Hiroshima'": DF/RH

"To Albert Einstein": DF/RH

"To Jonathan Swift": CM/RH

"To Laura": DF/RH

"To Myself, for an Album, New Year's 1950": DF/RH

"To Tadeusz Różewicz, Poet": DF/RH

"Treatise on Morals": DF/RH

"Two Men in Rome": DF/ RH

"Untitled": DF/RH

"The People's Graphic Workshop": DF/RH

"You Who Wronged": RL